Spying

on the

Enemy's

Camp

Spying

on the

Enemy's

Camp

by Sal Dena

with Laura England

Huntington House Publishers

Huntington House Publishers
P.O. Box 53788
Lafayette, Louisiana 70505

Library of Congress Card Catalog Number 93-78890
ISBN 1-56384-053-7

All Scripture quotes taken from The New King James
Version c. 1982 by Thomas Nelson Publishers

It wasn't easy for Christ to die on the Cross either. A word, a shrug, or a flick of His wrist could have arrested the whole procedure, and He could have saved Himself. He didn't, and now we have freedom from slavery to that abomination. Satan hates the Cross, and what he wants out of you is for you to hate it as well. He has two avenues for you to go to help him reach his goal. His ego is served by the flamboyancy of those who outwardly excoriate the Son of God and worship his name. His purposes are served by those who sheepishly adhere to the dos and don'ts of Christian culture and hate God with every rebellious thought and act.

Sal Dena has something to say to people who take either one of these paths in their service to Satan. He's here to tell this story because someone's courtship with rebellion might be derailed as a result of it.

Now a word about basing a book on criminal activities. Some of the cases on which Sal Dena has worked or assisted in the investigation are still open, officially unsolved. These, while mentioned and discussed here, will seem to be missing information, necessarily so. It is not the authors' intention to unduly accuse any person of doing something that has not been substantiated in a court of law; therefore, details will appear to be lacking.

In addition, as a detective Sal has had to use methods in obtaining information that might not be considered standard police procedure. That's why he's a private detective and not a police officer. That's also why there might appear to be gaps in some of the stories we tell here—he just can't let all of his secrets be known.

Finally, both Satan and God see you as a significant participant in the Great Plan. How do we know this? You wouldn't be reading this book if God Himself had not wanted it to happen. That's how significant you are to His plan. But for the Son of God, none of this could have been accomplished.

NOTE: You will notice that a number of the quotes used to open the chapters come from the pen of C.S. Lewis. Clive Staples Lewis was a writer/theologian whose significant impact upon Christianity practiced with a biblical world view began in the first part of this century. Throughout his classic pieces of Christian literature, his healthy respect for God's plan of redemption and use of forces good and evil to bring this about is evident. Readers of Lewis know that references to Satan and devils can be found in his writings about the culture (*The Abolition of Man, Mere Christianity*), his countless correspondences with friends, students, and peers (*Letters to an American Lady*), or his fictionalized accounts of the battle between good and evil written for both children and adults (*The Narnia Chronicles, The Space Trilogy*). This is because as a humble student of the Bible and the culture, C.S. Lewis was well aware of the truism that in order to defeat one's enemy, one must know one's enemy. His is a method of study we should all emulate, beginning with the Word of God.

—— * ————————————————————————————————

Dedication

I would like to dedicate this book to the families and loved ones of all the victims mentioned in this book and all the other victims whom I omitted for various reasons. May God continue to comfort you in your pain and suffering as you draw nearer to Him. Remember, God takes note of all our wanderings and gathers all our tears in a bottle (Ps. 56:8).

—— * ——————————————————————————————

Contents

Preface

After twenty years as a licensed private investigator into the occult, Sal Dena still finds it difficult to define satanism, the occult, or witchcraft. The list of elements that can be a part of any situation where the occult or satanism has played a role is endless, and no single incident ever reflects every item on the list. Very often it turns out to be an inexplicable combination of symbols, evidences, activities, and beliefs.

Combine this with the desperate need for secrecy most participants of the black arts demand (particularly the most violent and deadly elements), and the job of a Christian attempting to expose them grows even more difficult. There is only one way Sal Dena believes he has been able to last this long in the field, being successful in solving occult-related crimes: The hand of God has guided him into this place of accomplishment.

Sal Dena has followed the milestones of the spiritual war begun in the Garden when Satan took on the identity of the serpent. God proclaimed then that "the seed of the woman would crush the head of the seed of the serpent" (Gen. 3:15). Sal knows the outcome of the battle as well. As Welsh revivalist author Mrs. Jessie Penn-Lewis reminds us in *War on the Saints*, "Satan triumphed; but God overruled. The victim is made the vehicle for the advent of a Victor, who should ultimately destroy the works of the Devil and cleanse the heavens and the earth from every trace of his handiwork."[1]

With the battle raging, and Satan and his minions laying out their plans to capture ground and take prisoners, Christians who know their duties take the Word of God in hand and heart and pursue the battle to the very entrance of Hell's gate. The fight begins with everyday living: affecting what is known as a biblical world view. Many believers are doing this already—fighting pornography in the neighborhood, rescuing babies doomed in abortion mills, sacrificing luxuries to send their children to Christian schools. Some take the call to more definitive action against the enemy and enter the ministry or journey to the mission field.

Then there are those few who go right into the heat of the conflict and become spies on the enemy's camp. Sal Dena is one of those. He has seen up close what happens when God's creation fraternizes with God's enemy. He has learned that there is only one way to prepare for this kind of warfare: submission to God and His Word. After doing a scholarly investigation of the occult, theologian Dr. Gary North noted in his work on the subject, *Unholy Spirits,*

> I have seen serious investigators turn into quasi-occultists themselves. They began to believe what the occultists claimed for themselves and their religion just because the investigators saw that the occultists could, in fact, display supernatural powers in certain instances. The manifestations of occult power (which are all too real) blinded the investigators to the misrepresentations of the nature and source of such power. They became hypnotized by Satan's power religion because they were not grounded in God's ethics religion.[2]

It's not going to be easy reading about some of the cases Sal has to report to the church detailing the activities of Satan and his followers. These are stories of despair, heartbreak, and horror; the players are real—not fictional characters or actors taking on roles. It is hard to look at the damage wreaked by a hate-filled opponent.

---- * --

Acknowledgments

I would be greatly amiss if I did not begin these acknowl-
edgments recognizing the work of my co-author Laura England. Despite the fact that she and I have never met face-
to-face, my wife and I feel as though we know her well as a
true Christian sister. Laura's professional assistance as a writer,
knowledge of the publishing field as an editor, and Christian
witness as a testimony to God's grace all contributed tangibly
to the production of this book, as well as intangibly to the
spiritual fervor and passion.

When I first spoke to Laura, she, as an editor, told me that
I needed someone to turn this story into a book. When I
returned to Huntington House a year later to tell them I
hadn't been able to find a writer and to ask if they would assist
me in locating one, it was to my great pleasure that I discovered
that Laura was now available as a writer to do that very thing.

As I now look at the finished product, I realize that when
it says "with Laura England" on the cover, it really means that.
The talent and skills she put into this project are barely covered by such a sparse acknowledgment.

Going back a bit further, before I even had anything to

turn over to my co-author, there were others who influenced me. Over the years several people, ranging from personal friends and family to pastors, from news persons to celebrities, have asked me if I would write a book on this subject. My answer was always the same: "If and when the Lord is ready to reveal this, He will let me know . . . until then, I am to occupy until He returns."

It was not until I was a guest on "Focus on the Family" that Dr. James Dobson added his name to that list and asked me if I would write a book. Later while we were on the air, during a break, he brought it up again. Finally at the end of the program, he said, "Well, Sal, how about that book?" I said, "Okay, I'll do it."

Thank you, Dr. Dobson, for your urging me to carry out my responsibility. Thanks also to your entire ministry, held in high esteem by me and thousands of truth-seeking believers worldwide.

I would also like to acknowledge my mother, who was steadfast in the Word enough to "train up this child in the way he should go." But I have another "mother" for whom I publicly express my appreciation, Bernice Olesberg, my dearly departed ex-mother-in-law, who succumbed to cancer about two years ago—what a dear saint. She urged me several times to write a book, but it was not reality until after her death.

Bernice and I had a wonderful and special relationship. Back in the early years when I was working narcotics, I would be troubled, not knowing where to look for answers. I would often attend family functions, present in body but not in spirit, with a thousand-yard-stare on my face and hurting deeply inside. No one else seemed to know, but she did. She often visited my home while I was not there, where she would look on my desk and see my notes to myself, pondering how I should handle this or that—cases, investigations, personal crises. She would leave notes too. "Try Proverbs 3:5,6." Or when she knew I was suffering, she would write, "Try Romans 8:18 and Romans 8:26."

This went on for a few years until I was united with her in the kingdom. She was the first one I called to tell of my conversion. I am sure that her rewards in heaven are stacked several miles high. I miss you, Bernice.

On Becoming a Spy

The word "deceived" is, according to Scripture, the description of every unregenerate human being, without distinction of person, race, culture, or sex.—Mrs. Jessie Penn-Lewis, *War on the Saints*

The thought of viewing a body has never been very appealing to me, but how else was I to determine the possibility of satanic or occult involvement lest I see the remains? Viewing the partial remains was always worse. This was an unfortunate aspect of my job, and there was no way I could prepare myself fully for the episode.

Most unsettling are the times when a body or body parts are discovered without anticipation—when I'm just poking around a site looking for clues and stumble on more than I'd bargained for. Then there is no opportunity to emotionally or mentally condition my senses for the sight, or smell.

Once I see with my own eyes the remains of a victim of violent crime, I always ask myself the same question, "What kind of an animal would do this to another human being? Surely no human could purpose to do something like this." Immediately, the recurring thought comes back to me that enables me to move forward on this (and other) investigation(s). "You can't use conventional investigative techniques to solve an unconventional crime. You must put yourself in the shoes of the criminal; you must think like him; you must be him."

It was a gray day in Seattle; a light drizzle was falling. I stepped inside the circle of police tape, my eyes on the picture in front of me. Only the heads of four female victims were found in this hidden, wooded location, all laid neatly in a row. The medical examiner said that all the heads had been removed from the torsos with one sharp chop. The bodies were not found anywhere in the area. He added that he believed it was a "ritual killing" and that the heads had probably been at the location for three or four months.

The standard police explanation was given to the press: animals had removed the bodies and limbs.

I knew the police didn't really believe their routine line, at least not this time, but it was something to tell the media. The demands of an investigation like this regularly included every attempt to curb possible hysteria. Sometimes, though, the authorities refuse to answer the media's questions altogether, which usually only instigates speculation. I've learned that no one is forcing me to answer yes or no to a question; there exist countless responses to most inquiries. Simply, one can always say, "We don't know; give us time to find out."

Only the comments of the medical examiner had to be kept quiet in this case. I went to work searching for clues, though none could be found. The elements and the woods' inhabitants had stripped the site of anything that might have once provided a peek at the mind behind this horrible act. I came up empty-handed. I would find out later that a police detective had found a macumba rite doll (like a voodoo doll) nearby.

Weeks passed, and there were disappearances of more young women—and some findings as well. Panic was firmly taking hold in the Northwest. Parents worried excessively whenever their daughters were ten minutes late from school or strange men appeared in their neighborhoods. The authorities wished they were endowed with extra arms to stave off frantic questions and the media's microphones and notebooks, and extra legs to put to work on the cases. Eventually, most of the missing cases would be attributed to convicted killer Ted Bundy. It is now known, however, that other ritualistic murderers were operating in the area.

The next discovery produced two torsos with one missing one arm and a leg from the opposite side of the body. The other was missing the opposite pair of limbs. Also found at that location was a leg of a third victim. I'd been doing this work for several years by this time; additionally, I'd spent time in narcotics work. Nothing split my gut more than this endless battle with a madman destroying the lives of young women. I pictured them in my mind, beloved daughters, sisters, and wives, laughing, animated faces, bright eyes. I envisioned them chasing their dreams, perhaps becoming doctors, teachers, engineers, mothers. I imagined them in the warm embraces of their families, loved, accepted, and protected. Only this time the arms of their families had not been long enough to reach out and shield them from this gruesome end.

I remembered the words of the medical examiner at the previous site—"ritual killing." What could he have meant by that? My occupation required me to think logically through everything, every clue, every interview with witnesses or suspects, every detail of a case. I couldn't do it if I started relying upon non-tangible speculation. Certainly there were times when I'd followed a hunch, but every hunch has a logical thread running through it. Ritual killings? There's nothing logical or rational about that.

What was most intriguing to me was the fact that no one was investigating why mutilations were taking place and what possible purpose they served. In those early stages, talk about ritual murder occasionally surfaced, but the murders of the four girls, as well as the countless other missing women in the northwest, were soon discounted by the police as the work of "crazies." Crazies, of course, meant people who had no preconceived purpose for mutilating the bodies and no intended or projected results—irrational, illogical behavior.

I began to read everything I could get my hands on regarding ritual murders, and there wasn't much available. I soon learned that the only place that I could find that kind of literature was in an occult book store or in the Holy Bible. There were historical books on the subject, but they too associated ritual murders to some kind of religious ritual. I concluded that I was dealing with the spiritual realm.

I remembered as a child in church and Sunday school that our missionaries to Brazil had come across ritual acts. Many involved the sacrifice of humans and animals to various gods, demanding appeasement or bribes to provide what the people desired: fertility, a good harvest, victory in warfare. The bloodletting and rituals always coincided with particular religious days.

The children sat on the edges of the pews as the missionaries recounted these events, and I was no less interested than the rest in the heart-stopping stories of their lives in the jungles of Brazil. This was another world to me.

Now, here, today in the sophisticated, culturally advanced United States, in my own city of Seattle, I was faced with very similar activities. What did those missionaries know that was still a mystery to me?

My progress was slow. I still believed I could approach this case from a purely rational, intellectual stance. Although I read the material and based my conclusions on historical and empirical evidence about Satan worship, I could not comprehend the value system with which I was faced. The battle was between Good and Evil, Light and Dark.

I began to study the Old Testament, focusing on passages about sacrifice to the gods of Baal, child sacrifice, snake worship, blood-letting, etc. I discovered the twelve hundred deities of the Egyptians and their penchant for a god for everything. The worship of false gods is nothing new; it has been around since almost the beginning of time. The Bible did provide more information to help me understand the history of sacrifice and Satan worship. Still, I had a problem: it was 1974, there were bizarre murders taking place, which I felt were ritualistic, and it was my job to find out who was committing them. What good would that information do me in solving these cases?

Certainly, I wouldn't have to get involved in this religious stuff to find my answers? With that thought, all my rationalism disappeared, and denial and rejection rose up out of my heart. I didn't want to become religious just to solve a case. For years I'd been running from God. During that time, people would ask me if I was a Christian, and I would come up with a flip answer like, "No not yet, I haven't made that commitment yet." I chose other things over Him.

I was eighteen, right out of high school, when I joined the marine corps. I no sooner got through basic training when the Cuban missile crisis broke out. I was in Cuba for the duration. I returned from the land of Fidel and was immediately shipped overseas to be stationed in Okinawa, Japan. Everyone in the military, and my base was no exception, had their minds on the problems in a little communist-held country called Vietnam.

That whole part of the world was ticking like a time bomb. Time was ticking for me, too; I had a month of duty left in Okinawa. Then Vietnam exploded.

I was on the *U.S.S. Valley Forge*, in convoy in the Gulf of Tonkin crisis, making our assaults via helicopter. The *U.S.S. Maddox* and the *U.S.S. Turner Joy* were fired upon by a Soviet P.T. boat on 7 August 1964. A week later, on the fourteenth, the United States retaliated and bombed some fuel bases in Vietnam.

I made some foxhole promises to God then. The Lord preserved me, but it took me a while to keep my end of the covenant; in fact, I went through a few years of the kind of living that I know grieved the Holy Spirit. It is this tendency of man to break promises that has kept him from being able to do anything about his own salvation. God has to keep our promises for us. He followed through with me after I'd returned to the States.

Then, as now, I was faced with some more hard evidences, which had to be dealt with, and I could see the writing on the wall. I would go no further unless I stopped seeing the world and the Creator of it on my terms and began working on these cases—and my life—on His terms.

This was the way God converted me. The Lord cornered me, gaining entrance to my life through this investigation. My work satisfied me so much, I would respond to anything that affected it. My skills were suddenly found lacking because of my godless world view. (Christ said that "he who is not with Me is against Me; and he who does not gather with Me scatters abroad" [Matt. 12:30].) To continue my pursuit of truth and excellence, I knew I would have to change my approach.

I finally came to grips with the real truth. I knew the only way I'd be able to "see" what was going on in the case would be to take on the "eyes" of God. I could only do that by letting him have my life. I did, and though it seemed to me that I didn't have much choice in the matter, I knew I'd been saved from an eternally terrible fate.

As I began to read the Bible, I realized that man had been presented with the opposing views of good and evil since the time of Adam and Eve. Man would never be able to escape the consequences of his sinful ways. That's what being dead in his sins means—thoroughly incapable of anything, let alone rousing himself to eternal life. After the Fall of Man in the Garden, all men were tainted by sin. How could he ever escape this fate? God provided a vehicle of mercy and grace through the death of his only Son, Jesus Christ, the only acceptable way to cleanse man from the sin of Adam. The mandate given by God is life, if he obeys in Christ, and death, if he disobeys in the flesh—in man.

Jesus said, "I know your works, that you are neither cold nor hot. . . . So then because you are lukewarm, and neither cold nor hot, I will vomit you out of My mouth" (Rev. 3:15,16). Pretty graphic language. But it is mild in comparison to the graphic demonstrations Satan makes in trying to convince the world of his power and evil. I found myself facing it more and more every day.

I began to go to my knees on a regular basis. As I was taught to pray by my mother years ago, I opened and closed my prayers with "if it be Thy will."

I knew one of the first things I'd have to commit to the Lord was my "tough guy" image. The ugliness of the inside was gone, but the worst caricature anyone could dream up of the loud mouth, heavy drinking, dry-eyed, hard-hearted ex-Marine was still on the outside. I went to my knees and asked God to soften my heart. I covenanted to God to never take a life without just cause (self-defense or in defense of my family).

"Father, if it be Thy will, use me as an instrument to accomplish your work. Never allow me to become headstrong and haughty. Keep me open-minded and teachable. And Lord, if this is your desire for me, I ask you to make me successful in this endeavor for your glory."

I asked God to help me hate the sin, but not the sinner. He made it happen. In the midst of my horror of the crimes, I took on caring for not only the victims and their families, but also the killer and his family. Their far removal from God's ways must have had them in mortal pain. Unbelievably, I found it possible to have tears again.

I've always thought of the phrase attributed to our relationship to Christ: He must be Lord of all or He is not Lord at all. Puritan writer John Milton wrote in his fabulous epic, *Paradise Lost*, that upon his exile from heaven, Satan cried out in anger, "Better to reign in Hell than serve in Heaven." There's really no middle ground for anyone.

As I began to grow spiritually, the Lord began to open my spiritual eyes and let me see things that were impossible to see before. His words promised me that he would direct me in my understanding of the caliber of this enemy with whom I was dealing. "Call to Me, and I will answer you, and show you great and mighty things, which you do not know" (Jer. 33:3). "The secret things belong to the Lord our God: but those things which are revealed belong unto us and to our children for ever, that we may do all the words of the law" (Deut. 29:29).

My heart was right; my eyes were on God; He was my meditation. Oh, how I love to reminisce of those first days.

God revealed more and more, but with those revelations came a tremendous amount of responsibility. This is maturity in the making. The line of communication between a heart for God and a mind trained to discern began to burn up with messages more than ever. My spiritual eyes had been opened. Clearly these bizarre cases were going to have to be approached with more than rational thinking. Being like-minded with Christ began to help. My thinking became refined and enhanced by my heart.

Things started happening. I began getting calls from those who had come out of the occult, satanism, and witchcraft through the power of Christ. The stories of their involvement were chilling at first, but I remembered, "Greater is He that is in me, than he that is in the world."

Finally I had contact with a prison inmate on death row in Idaho who claimed to be involved in some ritual killings in the Seattle area. Thomas Eugene Creech, a mass murderer who had made similar claims to the Seattle police before, told a King County police officer that he had been present in a house when four women were decapitated. He described the victims, a house in Burien near the airport, and how to get there. He said the authorities would find a wishing well in the front yard, and at the back of the house, by the kitchen, there would be a stairwell going to the basement. At the bottom of the stairs on the right would be the "black" room. The south wall would have a pentagram on it, and the west wall would have blood splatters all over it. That was where he alleged the decapitations took place.

I had heard about the interview and waited for the police to take action. Word got around that there would be no investigation. How could that be? I thought. Creech has assisted countless federal, state, and local agencies all over the country solve open murder cases. Why wouldn't the Seattle police take advantage of this tip? I couldn't believe the answer I'd overturned when I started nosing around. A Creech tip several years ago had left the police empty-handed after they searched Lake Washington for a number of male bodies Creech had claimed he dumped there. The bodies were not found; therefore Creech was branded a liar.

This carte blanche rejection of his tip just because of an earlier embarrassment baffled me. The lake is enormous, I thought, I would have been more surprised if they had found the alleged bodies. And what's to lose? Looking through a house is certainly less involved than searching a lake.

Going on the information I had obtained (surreptitiously) from that interview I located the house. It was a HUD house, boarded up tight. I contacted the Seattle police homicide and intelligence units, who were working on the Missing Women of the Northwest Task Force, which included this case. I told them I found Creech's house and I wanted to go in. We met near my office and went over there together.

We found the wishing well outside and the stairwell in the back of the house next to the kitchen. Equipped with hammers and crowbars, we tackled the boards. I was the first one in and followed the route that Creech said we should take to the "black room."

We cautiously approached the basement. The "black room" was at the bottom of the stairs. My heart inched toward my throat. I was struck by how cold and desolate the place seemed. What a terrible place to die. Painted black—walls, ceilings, and floor—it had all the characteristics of a tomb.

There it was, just as Creech had said. The image was so gruesome, it is difficult to remember if it filled the room, or if it only seems that way now in my memory. A large pentagram was painted on the south wall. Dried blood was splattered on the west wall. Not blood stains, blood splatters, as if they had struck the wall with a great deal of force. As if, possibly, the blood had spurted forth after a deadly blow to the neck, forceful enough to separate the head from the torso.

The King County police lab technician took samples of the dried blood with a swab, and we later found out that it was not only human blood, but there were four different blood types on the wall. The police never did reveal whether or not the blood was of the same type as the victims.

I later interviewed the neighbors across the street who had claimed the house was visited regularly by what they described as "very strange people". They reported to me that they also detected some putrid aromas drifting from the house, and the inhabitants made several trips to the dump with large, sealed-up plastic bags. Then there was the night a girl's screams split the damp, dark air. "Help, help me, please, somebody help me," they heard coming from the house. Other neighbors confessed to being afraid of the couple living there. It was known in the community that the people who lived in the house with the "black room" were involved in the occult.

Finally the couple moved out, sneaking away in the middle of the night, leaving piles of garbage by the curb. Such a horrendous odor began to fill the neighborhood, and dogs started to get into the bags, that the neighbors had the load hauled away. This was all months before the police searched the house, but after Creech had made his claim. No one had looked inside the bags.

Some police detectives did not agree with my conclusions because they felt that I put too much faith in the words of a convicted killer. But my confidence in his testimony came from more than hearsay. I had met Thomas Creech when I received a telephone call from a friend of mine, an ex-FBI agent who was now an attorney working with Christian prisoners. He told me that Creech had become a believer in prison, and that he had told Creech about me and my work on the case of the four dead girls. He said he'd encouraged Creech to work with me. The prisoner agreed, realizing he had a duty as a believer to come forth . . . he had nothing to lose.

One of the most difficult things for a nonbeliever to understand is the fact that once a person accepts Christ, "old things are passed away, and all things become new." God throws our sins into the sea of forgetfulness and remembers them no more. Thomas Eugene Creech tried to right as many wrongs as he could, helping authorities throughout the midwest in closing unsolved cases; many of those law enforcement leaders considered him an expert in the area of the occult.

He stuck by his story about killings in the Seattle area and insisted they were all motivated by Satan worship and committed during satanic rituals. He offered to lead police to gravesites where sacrifice victims had been buried. But still the police rejected any assistance he could offer, refusing to believe Creech was anything but an unreliable source, denying his ability to assist.

The last piece of evidence Creech put forth was that Ted Bundy had been present at many of the rituals, including the decapitations of the four girls.

As an investigator, I don't take things at face value, I always "test the spirits." But I also keep in mind that there are often more than simple answers to any puzzle. God opened my eyes, exposed hidden information, and led me to important clues. I was delighted to have this new world view and happy to give God the glory. The unwilling attitudes of the authorities disappointed me, but I knew it was to be expected as long as their eyes were blinded. They simply couldn't see with the spiritual eyes I'd gained.

I began to get more and more homicide and narcotics investigations involving the occult, satanism, and witchcraft. Referrals poured in from attorneys, police officers, church groups, and by word of mouth. In 1975, I began receiving several requests for speaking engagements. I also started taking cases involving religious cults. Deprogrammings became a common service at Sal Dena Private Detective, Inc.

The end result was that I was spending more time in the word, being prepared for an even greater task the Lord had for me. It was the only kind of preparation that would adequately open my eyes for the work I was doing. It was in God's own school of discipleship that I learned how to survive in this ministry. (To be in ministry, you don't have to be a minister. Even as an investigator, I had a God-ordained task that contributed to God's goal of building the kingdom.)

By this time, there was no doubt in my mind that God had heard and answered my prayers. I know God was using me by the fact that I began to suffer—my health and my marriage both felt the burning arrows sent from the enemy's camp. Demons were at work, but I didn't recognize it at the time. Until then, I had never really encountered any real oppression, and why should I? I had never before done anything to harm Satan and his kingdom.

As my growth continued, I realized that Satan doesn't really concern himself with those who are not doing him harm; the ones who threaten him are those he wants to devour. Those who already belong to him are on a collision course.

"Fear not; for I am with you: be not dismayed; for I am your God: I will strengthen you; yes, I will help you; I will uphold you with My righteous right hand. . . . For I the Lord your God will hold your right hand, saying to you, 'Fear not; I will help you'" (Isa. 41:10,13).

A Good Spy Scope

> From ghoulies and ghosties and long-legged beasties
> and things that go bump in the night, Good Lord,
> deliver us!—Old Scottish prayer

Satan Who?

It's always been said that there are two things one should never bring up in polite company—religion and politics. I'd like to add one more topic to that short list: Satan.

The days are long gone when stories of a red-skinned, long-tailed, horned devil were told to naughty little children, hopefully scaring them into obedience. I doubt if many marketing or advertising agencies would be willing to introduce even a cute little demon as a part of a logo or marketing campaign—it just doesn't sell anymore.

Advertising has always been a fickle game, but it's not only in commercials or on billboards that the caricature has become scarce. The whole image of the Devil as a tangible being who pesters even the best of us has changed.

Today, bringing up Satan in polite conversation can get you one of two reactions: either skeptical mutterings about superstitious holdovers from the medieval days, or anticipation of stories of gory and graphic possession, obsession, and mayhem, barring no gruesome or graphic detail.

For proof of the first response, go to any of the major bookstore chains, pick up a book on business management, the arts, the environment, education, or religion, and there's a good chance the authors will attempt to introduce you to a modern-day paganism. The upshot is a neutralization of your image of Satan, conforming it to one that pairs him closely with Jesus Christ Himself. Life to such self-righteous, enlightened writers is so much more palatable when people worry less about the bad things they do and focus more on the good (or god) in man. Look out for the condescending commentary on traditional, orthodox Christianity's backwards, unprogressive, paranoid philosophy depicting Satan as the enemy of God.

The view of devils and demons is wide-ranging, and the minions of Satan know their influence depends upon how man sees them. C.S. Lewis' book of fantastical correspondence between a senior demon, Screwtape, and his novice nephew, Wormwood, supposes what lessons an experienced tormentor of man might teach his anxious charge. In the preface of *The Screwtape Letters*, Lewis states:

> There are two equal and opposite errors into which our race can fall about the devils. One is to disbelieve in their existence. The other is to believe, and to feel an excessive and unhealthy interest in them. They themselves are equally pleased by both errors, and hail a materialist or a magician with the same delight.[1]

Magicians, in particular practitioners in the black arts, are not the only ones overly interested in devils. Much of society has a tweaking little desire to know more about this forbidden topic. This is evidenced by the number of daytime talk shows and prime-time "reality" shows that spotlight everything from self-proclaimed witches whose motives are "good" to exorcisms of demons that cause their hosts to snarl and foam at the mouth to violent occult groups that actually perpetrate chaotic crime.

Our society has become so attuned to vivid pictures of

death, chaos, and evil that it takes increasingly vivid, more
realistic images to maintain the level of titillation. It is accepted among researchers who study the effects of pornography on men, and subsequently women, children, and society
in general, that a pattern almost without fail develops in the
individual who views pornographic images—much the same as
the physiological process of alcohol intoxication. A first drink,
a first viewing of "soft porn" (when the subject is partially
clothed), is at first very effective in achieving the desired result: a buzz or arousal, respectively.

Having one drink or one peek every night begins to have
a different effect—that is of none at all. The buzz is dimin-
ished. They are the same old pictures over and over again. (So
what if it's a different girl this time, the degree of disrobing
is the same.) The next step depends upon the potentiality for
addiction. If the individual plateaus here, he may be somewhat
arrested in his maturity, but he's probably safe from the dan-
gers of excessive imbibing. However, if he's inclined to believe
he needs more, he'll move on to the next stage, and then the
next and the next.

Extensive documentation exists that demonstrates a significant tie between heavy drinking and high incidence of
automotive fatalities, and overindulgence in viewing pornography and perpetration of violent sexual crime. With such pat-
terns of "intoxication" available for review, and with our knowledge of the nature of unregenerate man, is it any wonder the
television dial is full of overindulgence in graphic, vivid messages, teasing society's opinions about Satan?

Of course, publicists—whose jobs are evaluated on how
many people they can get to watch a program—are not completely lacking in functioning cerebral cells. The promos will
always say the purpose of the programming is to assist you in
being able to detect the evil when it is near; to protect you and
your family; to expose these dastardly wicked elements of the
world. This way both they and you can feel good about par-
ticipating in such a socially positive activity as watching a
gratuitously graphic program. In truth you are in search of
titillation, and the broadcasters are paying homage to the god
called ratings.

What does all of this have to do with Satan? While he might not serve as an appropriate topic for enlightened conversation, he certainly finds his way into the theme of many television programs. This can only be accomplished if it's what the broadcasters believe the viewers want to see. Satan has become a hidden, forbidden fruit. No one would admit to being as tantalized by the stories of demonic possession, satanic worship, witchcraft, and wizardry as their viewing habits might portray. But who's watching when we watch?

Sadly, Christians seem to have become more addicted to sensational accounts of the Devil's activities than any other group. With untrained overemphasis in the community of the church on what Satan is up to and the unfortunate lack of devotion to knowing God, there's little wonder there are now attempts in Christian media and publishing to balance reports of satanic ritual abuse or demon possession with charges of hysteria (to be discussed more thoroughly in chapter 8). The unfortunate results of this paradoxical combination of preoccupation and "investigative reporting" may backfire and convince the church that a more frivolous, light-hearted approach to the viper of the underworld is warranted.

With constant exposure to the elements of Satan's dark kingdom, I know God had placed a hedge of discernment and protection around me to prevent my succumbing to the temptations of the sensational aspect of the work. It has nothing to do with any strength I have; as Christ promised, where I am weak, He is strong. I've been approached by numerous media outlets and associations and asked to speak about my work. Some have specifically requested that I focus on the gory details of my most exciting cases. I wouldn't, and their disappointment was obvious.

Scopes and Sights

My understanding of satanism, the occult, and witchcraft may be somewhat different than that of numerous other credible and often more highly trained authorities. As I've mentioned previously, though, my school of learning has been in the field. In order to be a spy on the enemy's camp and survive, I've had to develop spiritual eyes. In addition, the tools of my trade include using a good scope: the method of surveying the field and taking count of the ammunition of the opposition. The Bible is the best scope I know to determine the truth about anything.

> Finally, my brethren, be strong in the Lord and in the power of His might. Put on the whole armor of God, that you may be able to stand against the wiles of the devil. For we do not wrestle against flesh and blood, but against principalities, against powers, against the rulers of the darkness of this age, against spiritual hosts of wickedness in the heavenly places. Therefore take up the whole armor of God, that you may be able to withstand in the evil day, and having done all, to stand. Stand therefore, having girded your waist with truth, having put on the breastplate of righteousness, and having shod your feet with the preparation of the gospel of peace; above all, taking the shield of faith with which you will be able to quench all the fiery darts of the wicked one. And take the helmet of salvation, and the sword of the Spirit which is the word of God; praying always with all prayer and supplication in the Spirit, being watchful to this end with all perseverance and supplication for all the saints—and for me [Paul], that utterance may be given to me, that I may open my mouth boldly to make known the mystery of the gospel, for which I am an ambassador in chains; that in it I may speak boldly, as I ought to speak. (Eph. 6:10-20)

Satanism is defined by the *American Heritage Dictionary, 2d College Edition*, as "the worship of Satan characterized by a travesty of the Christian rites."[2] Satanism could not exist without God. We know historically that Satan, as a creature, endeavored to surpass in power and devotion the Creator. All that Satan does is wrapped up in the workings of the Creator, his enemy. His existence is not independent of God. There could be a God without Satan; there could have been no Satan without God.

This presupposition, defining Satan in the context of God, is the first great offense to our enemy. Imagine the pride and self-absorption that drove Satan to rise up in rebellion against the Almighty Maker. His temptation of man dwelt on the neutralization of God, so that he (Satan) might be perceived as more important than he was: "you will be like God," he said to Eve—as if being like God were attainable! Surely his gut wrenches every time a believer demands, "Get thee behind me, Satan!" in the name of Jesus, for he knows that he must do so, slinking away like a dog with his tail between his legs.

He exists only because God is tolerant of him. His very power has been granted to him by God. Remember the conversation between God and Satan over the righteousness of Job? Satan could do nothing to harm Job beyond the hedge God had drawn around his servant.

Traditionally, Satan has been accepted as the primary leader against God among non-believers. Many practice their rebellion in a variety of ways, sometimes never directly focusing on Satan himself; still such groups officially belong to the realm of the occult. The occult is recognized as activities which are hidden (the actual meaning of the word "occult") from the rest of the world and very often rooted in cultures where the gospel has not been heard. Therefore, neither do these cultures have the news about Satan. (Remember the missionaries to Brazil?) The practices of occultism center on searching out the unseen, using such techniques as divination, clairvoyance, magic, and spiritism, all "available only to the initiate,"[3] says the *American Heritage Dictionary*. In a slightly different vein, followers of New Age deities, self-deification, and paganism are all partaking in variances of anti-God occult religions—but it is all the same rebellion. This diversity and the hidden nature of the occult makes it very difficult to create a definitive sketch of the typical Satanist or occultist.

An even more slippery characterization is that of witchcraft and witches. Subsequent to years of reruns of Samantha the T.V. witch, and the recent film comedies of Hollywood, the task of convincing the public that witches exist—not only that they exist but that they may actually be among the bad guys—is nearly impossible. The dictionary definition of a witch is "a woman who practices sorcery or is believed to have dealings with the devil."[4] That doesn't sound like Dorothy's Glinda the Good Witch to me.

If witches weren't tough enough to nail down with clear identification, the dictionary defines witchcraft as "black magic; sorcery. A magical or irresistible influence, attraction, or charm."[5] Unfortunately, that could describe a wide spectrum of people or activities. In light of this, it's understandable that civil libertarians are worried when people or groups who identify themselves as Satan worshippers or witches are connected to illegal activity without compelling evidence. After all, worshipping Satan is not illegal (under U.S. laws, that is, not God's laws).

This constitutional protection is solid as long as the violence of satanic or occult activities remain in the closet. To their advantage, practitioners have been able to keep the worst, perhaps most offensive aspects of the occult hidden, so curious thrill-seekers encounter only the mystical, sensual elements of the practices. Thus, they are easily lured to become more involved. As the participation increases, in particular in a structured group or coven, more of the details are revealed. Finally, the threats begin. No one gets this far into the occult without making a life commitment; primarily because the truth is now out in the open: it is understood that few escape the occult alive.

Deception

One of Satan's greatest feats of deception has been to convince so many that he is more powerful than God, that evil is stronger than good. His mission is to convince believers and non-believers alike that his power is great enough to destroy the hold Jesus Christ has on the world. Satan's appeal therefore is that winners are on his team—a good recruiting ploy for one who needs a multitude of workers to accomplish his goal. But this scenario relies upon the necessity of cooperation among Satan's followers. History shows that chaos follows sinners everywhere. It is not likely that even Satan could keep his followers so cohesive and single-minded to be successful in wresting power from God. The only way he can accomplish anything here on earth is when God allows it, and when men believe Satan's lies—especially the lies that raise him and his evil ways over God and His goodness.

Anton LaVey's Satanic Bible provides a view of Satan that defines him not as a being but as a representation of a metaphysical state: what man's highest potential could be. Followers of all satanic philosophies are motivated by promises of physical gratification, satisfying the flesh and the ego, and power. Early worship of Satan was prominent among the lower classes; it was considered a form of rebellion against authorities, in essence against oppressors (God and the church, the latter admittedly not always having been the purveyors of morals and values in the community, particularly in early Christendom). There was a popular institution of a mock "Black" mass which blasphemed God and substituted demonic elements for the church's rituals. It has been romanticized among recruiters as the religion of revolution, providing justification for illegal activity. (Impressive review and analysis of the historical and cultural significance of occultism in the West is provided in theologian Dr. Gary North's revised book, *Unholy Spirits*.)

Thrill-seekers

Part of the deception includes variations in practice and terminology from group to group. The largest percentage of participants in occult activity are what are known as dabblers, and there is little consistency from individual to individual or cult to cult in activities. These are usually teen-agers who respond to that initial temptation of the forbidden fruit and enjoy the thrill of rebellion, of doing something parents, teachers, and other adults "don't understand." At this level, the involvement is mostly in "harmless" fun and games, and the vehicles through which participants enter this stage are areas of entertainment: heavy metal music, fantasy games or books, posters, and symbolism. So many youth look to their peers for approval, and taking on these behaviors assure acceptance into an exclusive group.

Generally, dabblers do not hold to any formal belief system. Theirs is an involvement of the senses. "I feel good when I do this, so I will do it." A manner of self-styled worship may develop from this stage, with minimal conscious adoption of the theology; still a heightened awareness that there is more to this than fun and games very often begins to take seed. A number of individuals plateau in this stage for a period of time, experimenting, looking for what works best for them.

A Growing Commitment

The next level of satanic activity demands more intellectual commitment and knowledge of specific teachings, usually variations on the Satanic Bible. A loosely structured group forms when individuals—usually dabblers—agree upon a set of beliefs and the acts required by the members to prove their devotion to the group or leader.

The obvious question is: If more mental exercise is demanded, why would teen-agers get more deeply involved? The adolescent years are generally accompanied by a general disassociation from societal elements, such as family, work, school, church. Initiative and effort are rare behavioral characteristics especially for teens whose involvement in satanic acts already demonstrates a tendency toward rebellion and lack of motivation. So how could teen-agers be worth the recruitment effort for a satanic group?

Remember the intoxication discussion from earlier in the chapter? When our thinking process and the actions that follow are so closely linked to how we feel about something, there is a chance of becoming addicted to the rush of feelings experienced. It is no different with teens and occultism. As the current level of thrill slowly takes on less excitement and becomes an old hat, the dabbler seeks more intoxicating titillation—something more forbidden, more dangerous, more powerful. The hardcore occult groups are waiting to take thrillseekers in at this stage.

A Hard Row to Hoe

Hardcore occultists have formulated a slightly more structured belief system which often includes a loose hierarchy, an initiation ritual, and some comprehension of the demands of traditional satanic worship. This group still lacks a real theological base and is motivated largely by self-gratification and power. They are more convinced than dabblers that secret, illegal, perverse, hedonistic behavior moves them up the ladder in Satan's kingdom, but less driven by a devotion to Satan than formal worshippers. Groups are disconnected and serve as a venue for bragging, baiting, and bullying. Still mostly populated by the young and disassociated, sophomoric acts and violence mix heavily with tough talk, and initiates are used to track and capture victims and dispose of bodies. Graverobbing, sexual assault, and animal mutilation are the crimes of choice. Murder (human sacrifice) is occasionally committed as a part of ritualistic practices.

Fine-tuned Satanism

Serious, highly structured worshippers of Satan are convinced of a particular theology about Satan (varying from group to group) and develop a rather sophisticated organization implementing symbols, holidays, literature, and rituals. Every group is specialized and reflects the character of the leadership and the members of the group. Just as college fraternities may adopt universally accepted beliefs but show variation in activities, hazing practices, and customs, so will satanic groups resemble one another in their intentions and opposition to God, but differ in elements of practice and worship.

Criminals and Grandfathers

Two other characteristics of occultists and Satanists thread their way through these representations. One is the criminally oriented individual. This is a person who believes that criminal action is the only way to achieve his or her goal and who finds an excuse in satanism. Their presence is found throughout all levels of satanic involvement.

The other is the intergenerational Satanist. As later chapters will show, I have taken on a number of cases where several members of the same family have been involved in occult activities. The Second Commandment forbids idol worship, and God's charge that the sins of the fathers shall visit upon the third and fourth generations has borne fruit. In addition, very often children are tormented by demons without the parents ever having been involved in satanism, but investigation shows ancestral worship of pagan deities.

Dr. C. Fred Dickason, chairman of the theology department at Moody Bible Institute and author of *Demon Possession and the Christian* and *Angels: Elect and Evil*, cites that in over five hundred cases studied, 95 percent reveal that there has been ancestral satanic activity. In a 1992 panel discussion on the radio program "Focus on the Family," Dr. Dickason stated that "if this activity is not interrupted, it will visit upon the next generation."[6]

Crime and violence do not necessarily occur at all levels of satanism, but anyone who deals with the two long enough knows where there's smoke there's fire. Law enforcement authorities advise their officers and any task forces or individuals investigating possibly occult-related crime to be aware of anything that could point them to illegal activity.

Discounting the thrill-seekers, those who participate in human sacrifice do so for a number of reasons. Some killings relate to the worship of Satan, others to the necessity of secrecy. Like the mafia, Satanists don't like big talkers, so many practices of satanism are never discovered. With the exception of cases when bodies are left behind because of a group's need to quickly evacuate the ritual site, illegal acts of satanic worship are made known only because the group has orchestrated a discovery: sometimes to taunt the authorities and frighten the community, sometimes to make a name for themselves, but most often to warn others. Either the victim had a problem keeping his or her mouth shut and was murdered to warn members, or the body was left as a message to other covens.

It is believed by hardcore Satanists that expelling the life of another serves as a pathway to more energy and power, which in turn assists the soul of the murderous Satanist toward greater purity and allegiance with Satan. An occultist willing to confess to two human sacrifices and now serving time for multiple counts of homicide made the following statement, published in a confidential law enforcement handbook, about the purpose of death in satanic worship:

> If you sacrifice an 80-year-old man, that is a nice sacrifice. If you sacrifice a woman, that is even better. The youngest female is the best sacrifice you could give. . . . We offer a child's spirit to Satan so if it grows

up in the spirit world, it can grow up to be what he wants it to be, to help.[7]

This murderer justified his actions with the demands of his religious expression and is convinced that his reward will be in his next life, when he will be reincarnated as rich and famous in appreciation for his work for Satan in this life.

The Philosophy of Sacrifice

Law enforcement authorities insist that the bizarre and grizzly scenes they encounter on the field are important to consider as part of satanic worship because so many of these groups take their religious activities so seriously. A study has been conducted within the penal system to lend some statistics to the research done on occult-related crime. Dr. Al Carlisle with the Utah State Prison System declares that in his interviews with Satan-worshipping inmates, their estimates of the numbers of sacrifices range from fifty thousand to fifty-five thousand per year.[8] Taking into account the likelihood that this is a vast over-exaggeration, it would still be shocking to consider even 10 percent of the fifty thousand, or 1 percent, take place. Five hundred human sacrifices per year allows for ten per state. Ten too many. (See chapter 9 for a discussion on the methods of sacrifice and abuse, necessary to dispel the criticisms of defenders of the freedom of Satan worshippers to express themselves. We may not be able to connect every element of Satan worship or occultism to a crime scene, but we certainly may report on what is found at crime scenes where rituals are known to have been performed, and let the reader draw his own conclusions.)

Parallels to Christianity

In order to maintain as much secrecy as possible and penetrate normal societal routines, occultists and Satanists will attempt to parallel accepted traditions or religious practices as much as possible. Of course every parallel is a perversion of the real thing, done with wicked gloating at the blasphemy against God. Opposites are the way occultists and Satanists attempt to set up a world antithetical to the one God created.

Since God is the God of order and truth, Satan's kingdom is to be chaotic and deceptive.

This is the blueprint for the followers of Satan. Much of the communications and symbolism of the occult have a pattern, but the pattern can only be detected once the order and truth of reality are abandoned as means of understanding. For example, a cross often appears among the items or markings of a ritual site, but the cross is always upside down—depicting the falseness of Christ's atonement or its inadequacy to redeem all men. Any symbol of death is used to denounce the gift of life graciously offered to children of God. The five-pointed star, or pentagram, serves as a popular and well-recognized occult symbol, in particular when positioned upside down as a baphomet. Words written in mirror image or with the letters backwards are common in occult writings or markings, such as N-A-T-A-S.

Holidays of the occult closely parallel the traditional holidays of orthodox Christianity, though of course the purpose for the celebration is quite different. Very often the theme of occult or satanic religious celebration are connected to blood letting (gathering power and energy) or sexual perversions. And without exception, the dates reflect traditionally pagan, especially pantheistic (nature-worshipping) events. Some of the most powerful days of the year are the spring and fall equinox and the summer and winter solstice. Five weeks and one day following each of these the sacrifice of a child of a Christian is required. Obviously, All Hallow's Eve, or Halloween, represents the highest holy day of satanism. These holidays demand the sacrifice of the purest, youngest virgin in homage to Satan. I've had psychologists, sociologists, law enforcement experts, and pastors from all over the United States relate stories to me—and they all resemble the descriptions of sacrificial rituals detailed in known satanic literature.

Sex and the Single Satanist

More extensive research has been done in the area of sexual abuse within the context of satanic practices than I could note in this book, especially in this chapter on the nature of satanism. This is also an area which those who charge that sensationalism and hysteria are more prevalent than incidents of satanic activity claim to be especially loaded with unsubstantiation, overwrought emotion, and gullibility.

Law enforcement authorities have no compelling reason to insert themselves in the theological debate—after all, for years they avoided investigating occult-related crimes because of the religious issue. Nonetheless, they are nearly unanimous nationwide in the acceptance of practices of occultism and satanism as a purpose in sexual abuse. Their handbooks on investigation of occult-related crime include entire sections on detecting, investigating, and interviewing satanic ritual abuse. Traditional occult literature insists on the sexual aspects of rituals to purify the commitment the members make to Satan.

Images and the Occult

Finally, investigative research done by Dr. Judith Reisman, who has no particular bone to pick with satanism, finds evidences of satanism throughout her studies of mainstream pornographic material. "Satanic photo stories glamourize tales of sexual demons,"[9] she says in her highly acclaimed book, *Soft Porn Plays Hardball*.

> Playboy found much humor in cartoons of very young girls who were ritualistically sacrificed. One such young girl is placed on a sacrificial altar, while another, waiting her turn to die, comments, "Takes some of the incentive out of being a virgin, doesn't it?"[10]

Reisman references the concerns raised by psychiatrist Linnea Smith in personal correspondence dated 11 April 1988:

> Public and professional concern is growing regarding ritualistic abuse cases. Bizarre and sadistic rituals, acted out as part of a cult, satanic church, coven, or other occult organization include systematic emotional, physical, and sexual abuse of infants, children, and adults. Linking religious, pseudo-religious, or supernatural symbols and ceremonies with the abuse of victims often involves wearing robes or costumes, drinking blood and urine, smearing feces, animal and human mutilation, multi-perpetrator, multi-victim sexual abuse, torture, and

homicide. These cartoons from *Playboy* magazine glamourizing and trivializing this type of activity for entertainment are unacceptable.[11]

Reisman references another scene found from her research, this one from *Playboy*'s December 1972 issue: "SCENE: A buxom woman lies on the sacrificial pyre when the chief of the tribe says, 'Are you guys nuts? The gods would never be this angry.'"[12]

This scene and the one referenced earlier are taken from what is known as soft porn—mainstream magazines accepted as less bizarre, perverse, or brutal in their photographic depictions than more explicit publications. Considering the extent of the child pornography industry and the insistence of cult groups on using the youngest and purest victims for sacrifice to Satan, it is not difficult to trace a link between pornography and satanism.

Dr. James Dobson, founder of the Christian, pro-family organization Focus on the Family, interviewed serial killer Ted Bundy just prior to his execution. Bundy confessed to being addicted to pornographic material at an early age. With my sources placing Bundy at the site of several sacrificial rituals, I can easily believe his testimony to being influenced by pornography. My question though is similar to that of the egg and the chicken: Which came first? I respectfully disagree with Dr. Dobson's conclusion that Bundy was influenced first by pornography. I am convinced his pornographic proclivities developed as a result of having turned his heart against God at an early age and over to Satan later in life.

Bundy's activity in the occult was not satanism, but a form of witchcraft and paganism. Some of the girls he murdered were found with teeth marks on the buttocks, typical of the markings I've seen when investigating pagan-related murders. Perhaps pornography assisted Bundy's paganism in neutralizing his feelings of inadequacy and isolation and gave him some models for destruction.

As will be seen in the following chapters, Satan works his wiles in a variety of ways. He taps into the desire for more power or thrill or sensual delight in some. In others, he sidles up to them in the midst of their "goodness" and promises "higher good." Says turn-of-the-century Welsh revivalist writer Mrs. Jessie Penn-Lewis,

> Goodness is, therefore, no guarantee of protection from deception. The keenest way in which the Devil deceives the world, and the Church, is when he comes in the guise of somebody, or something, which apparently causes them to go God-ward and good-ward.[13]

No other method of detecting the depravity of the world is as reliable as God's scope, the Bible. And man in all of his attempts to strive for goodness will find deception.

> "For My thoughts are not your thoughts, nor are your ways My ways," says the Lord. "For as the heavens are higher than the earth, so are My ways higher than your ways, and My thoughts than your thoughts." (Isa. 55:8,9)

God's word is the only means available to man to comprehend goodness and truth, and our successes will eventually dry up as long as our scopes are out of focus. I measure everything I uncover; I test the spirits, not only because as an investigator I need to thoroughly overturn every stone, but because I may otherwise waste my time searching with my natural eyes, instead of my spiritual eyes.

These are the things I learned when I started looking at my cases through a good scope. As I took on more jobs, my vision sharpened even more.

Catching the Copycat

[D]ivination, spirit-questing, magic, and witchcraft . . . represent efforts to have the future on other than God's terms, to have a future apart from and in defiance of God.–R.J. Rushdoony, *The Institutes of Biblical Law*

The Ted Bundy murder cases, originally the Missing Women of the Northwest case, started in 1974. The name of the investigation changed when reports of a guy named Ted started showing up, placing him at the locations where a number of the women had last been seen. The suspect usually had his arm in a sling, playing on the sympathy of the victims. Ted Bundy was the prime suspect.

A number of the cases I investigated at the time involved missing women, and that variable always forced me to consider that this might be another "Ted" case. Though I followed through on a number of trails and took on several cases during this time, most women were found missing for other reasons, including running away from home. It turns out that I never took a missing person case that began with no suspect and ended up with Ted Bundy as the known or suspected killer.

   This does not include the time I was retained by an affluent and prominent family to investigate Ted Bundy. Widely
connected and extremely wealthy, though not victimized by
the loss of a family member, they were simply distressed by
the pain and anguish suffered by their Northwest neighbors.
They wanted to see an end to the worrying.

   I began by interviewing all of the families of missing girls.
In Ellensburg, Susan Elaine Rancort disappeared from Central
Washington College. According to her companion, who es-
caped, a young man who said his name was Ted approached
her in the library and asked Susan Elaine to help him carry
books to his car. His VW was parked behind the library, and
the backseat upholstery was torn. This matched the description of Ted Bundy's vehicle. Though her friend got away,
Susan Rancort was not so fortunate.

   Neither was I in my investigation. There simply was not
enough evidence to place Ted Bundy at the scene of this
disappearance. I kept up with the case through contact with
other police departments nationwide, and agonized over the
disappearances of a number of young girls who were last seen
within fifty miles of my office.

   Through the first part of 1974, Bundy was brought in for
questioning on a regular basis by a staff of investigators made
up by King County police, Seattle police, state police, and the
organized crime unit. Every time a girl went missing and any
compelling evidence pointed to Bundy, back in he would be
for more questions about his whereabouts. The task force was
driven to irrationality with despair and frustration, trying
anything and everything to solve these cases.

   At one interview session, Bundy was being his charming,
pleasant, outgoing, confident self. He insisted he had never
done anything wrong; he accepted our apology for disturbing
him and eventually discovering the error of our ways. It happened that a clairvoyant was also in the building, offering her
assistance in locating "Ted." She took a composite that had
been drawn, put a hole in the top and ran a thirteen-inch
string through it. There, in the middle of the Seattle police
department, she bent at her waist, put one end of the string
to her forehead, and twirled the paper around.

"I will tell you where he is," she prophesied. When the twirling came to a stop, she flung her arm out toward the right and shouted, "There he is! Go get him!" It was all I could do to stifle a laugh.

I hesitate to hold the task force in too much disdain for relying upon the chicanery of charlatans like this woman. There were daughters and sisters and cousins and wives disappearing from what had once been considered safe havens: libraries, college campuses, neighborhood stores. The accountability of the police was under question because they couldn't track down this one man who was managing to make himself known to a lot of residents of the Northwest. Something had to be done.

I had a call from the parents of another young woman who was missing from the Seattle area. The local police were searching for a man who was her neighbor and also an escapee from a mental institution in the Midwest. His name was Gary Addison Taylor, and several months before the young housewife disappeared, he had returned from the Northwest to his then-current home and job in Detroit, Michigan, with his arm in a sling. Though Taylor was thirty-nine and the police believed he was too old to be "Ted," his movements seemed to parallel with the locations where a number of the Missing Women of the Northwest had disappeared.

Nearly three months had passed since Vonnie Stuth's disappearance, and the police had no fresh clues to her whereabouts. Her mother decided to hire me for two days to see if there were any areas that might have been overlooked. Her nineteen-year-old daughter was last seen at her own home the day before Thanksgiving. She had been married only five months.

The "leads had run out," Vonnie's mother, Lola Linstad, told me. "I don't know how to say this," she admitted to the press after Taylor was found and directed police to her daughter's burial spot, "because I know the police have done all they can, but I feel that the case was somehow shelved. . . . When you're waiting, you get anxious for information. The county told me they could not concentrate on Vonnie, that they had other cases to investigate."[1]

I knew little about this when I started the investigation. The first day on the job, over two months after her disappearance and the police inquiry, I went to the last home Taylor had rented in the suburb of Enumclaw, expecting to find very little this far into the case. The house was empty and clean. In the detached, double-car garage, there was a room about twelve-by-twelve feet. There was human feces in the corner, several empty bags from fast food outlets, and over two hundred cigarette butts on the floor—Doral brand, Vonnie's brand.

In the main garage were two 9mm. cartridge casings and five large, sealed, black plastic bags filled with garbage. After a few moments of digging, I concluded that the garbage belonged to Taylor. I lugged all the bags to my car and took them home to inspect them more closely.

It's a respected detective tip that one can discover a great deal about a person by inspecting his garbage. (Think now what you've recently tossed in the kitchen pail, or the trash can by your desk, and you'll know what I mean.) I waded my way through the usual collection of (quite pickled) foodstuffs, wrappers, torn envelopes from creditors, and bits and pieces of household throwaways, brokens, and scraps.

Then I unearthed a gem and began constructing a case against Taylor. Several hours later, I had pieced together four letters Taylor and his wife had written. One of the letters said that he was taking "the girl" with him to Portland, along with his armalite (.22 fold-up rifle). He indicated that he had to pick up some money and, later, renew the Michigan tags on his car.

I went to Vonnie Stuth's mother with my discovery, and Mrs. Linstad asked me to continue my investigation.

Taylor also mentioned in his correspondence that he had to store some things in his van at the rental house in Portland. A U-haul stub was found in the garbage, and after checking with the U-Haul office, I was given an address on North Calvert. Locked in the garage at the house there, which was discovered later to have been rented by Taylor's wife, was his van.

Because the police had not gathered enough compelling evidence to arrest Taylor, neither had they followed leads to this house, so the van had not been searched. I stopped to think a moment. Taylor had not been seen for several weeks and probably was not keeping up with routines of life, like paying bills. The van was a GM vehicle. On a long shot, I called the GMAC financing department and hit pay dirt. They wanted to repossess the vehicle; I wanted to search it. It was an easy trade.

After the van was removed and put into storage, I went through it. My searches continued to bear fruit. I found some long, light-brown hair which proved to be a perfect match to the hair found in Vonnie Stuth's hairbrush at her home. There were receipts noting the purchase of car insurance and payment of fees for a Michigan driver's license in Taylor's name.

I turned everything I found over to the county authorities except the cigarette butts and the spent rounds. I've never withheld anything from the police, particularly when they asked, but there was still detective work to do and I wasn't sure the police had proven themselves in this case to be keeping up on all the leads. They didn't ask, so I held on to it.

No question about it, the police had not investigated the disappearance of Vonnie Stuth thoroughly. Those garbage bags had been sitting in the garage for over four months, and no one had ever gone through them! I had no desire to embarrass or see egg on the face of the police; a cooperative working relationship with the local authorities was important to the success of my work, not to mention more glorifying to the God whom I served. I could not neglect what was plain to see though: not enough effort had gone into the case of this missing young housewife.

A few weeks after I'd passed the evidence over to the county, my office was broken into. There was no damage, nothing missing except for a brown paper bag with cigarette butts and two 9mm. casings in it.

It was over two years later when I found out that a saliva test had been done on the cigarette butts, and the blood type detected in the dried saliva was a direct match to Vonnie Stuth. How had this been done if I'd never given the materials to the police? My two-year-old suspicions were satisfied. A friend with King County police asked me if I remembered the case and the missing evidence. He confessed that he knew someone from his department had stolen the cigarette butts. Then he told me about the saliva test. Why didn't this come to light earlier? Probably because I wasn't making an issue out of it, and the police were waiting for the other shoe to drop, anticipating my making some statements to the press about the ineptitude of the police. I never did.

I must always remind people who would take up an offense for me when I've been robbed of any glory or recognition for my work on a case that I can't be robbed of something that's not mine in the first place. The glory and recognition belong to God. If I'm not there to collar the criminal, or ride master over the operations of the investigation, it does not matter to me. My job is to aid in detection. The Lord benefits when I do it properly.

Probably the most important find was a slip of paper noting three personal references for Taylor. One of the names was that of Dr. Richard Miller, the highest ranking witch in the northwest. The moniker was dubious to say the least but attributable as a result of some articles that had been printed in a couple of feature magazines published in the Northwest. Miller was teaching classes in the occult and witchcraft at the University of Washington experimental college during the summer months. He taught over thirty-seven classes under the guise of parapsychology.

A completely unexpected piece of the puzzle fell into place. Thomas Eugene Creech, the death row prisoner in Idaho, had claimed to have taken classes from this witch, along with Ted Bundy. Now we had three mass murderers under the tutelage of the same teacher, a witch. More startling leads were coming to light. The occult relationships among the three killers, as well as Taylor's bizarre activities, were beginning to squint from the beams of truth that flickered through the darkness.

According to a Detroit newspaper, Taylor had killed over two hundred people. He had been known as the "Sniper of Royal Oaks" and the "Bus Stop Sniper" in his early twenties when for three months he terrorized a community by sniping at women and girls with a .22 caliber rifle. He confessed to the incidents, was charged, then ruled insane and unfit to stand trial. He was admitted to a Michigan psychiatric hospital, where he was out of society's way for four years.[2]

In 1961, on one of his frequent leaves from the clinic, Taylor attacked two women with a machete. He was confined again to the hospital until 1966 when he was considered fit to face the sniping charges. The judge ruled him not guilty by reason of insanity. Taylor was returned to the psychiatric hospital and began being granted brief periods of leave in the summer of 1971. Then in the summer of 1972, he was given convalescent leave; the terms of the leave meant he had to report to the hospital once a month. Within a year he started neglecting the terms—his wife called the first time and said that Taylor was not feeling well. Then he never checked in at the clinic again. Women began disappearing from the Michigan area shortly afterward.[3]

The Detroit News described his previous home in Onsted, Michigan, as having a torture chamber in the basement. A friend of two Toledo, Ohio, women who had gone missing peeked in the windows of the home and spotted chains, manacles, sexual gadgets, and low, overhanging pipes. The police investigation revealed that the pipes and a pole had flesh hanging from them. There was also dried blood all over; an attempt to disguise the blood had been made by someone sweeping blue paint over the area.[4]

This man had to be caught soon, I knew, as it was just a matter of time before he would have to satisfy his insatiable thirst for blood again.

I knelt before the Lord for divine guidance. I told him how badly the families were feeling—though I knew He had already felt their pain—and how badly I hurt over this situation. I was reassured by the knowledge of the word that, however badly we hurt, He hurt that much more. He was the one that was personally acquainted with sorrow and grief.

As I look back now, I recall it was a long, grieving process for me, because I could not promise that if I caught Taylor, I would not kill him. I had promised God I would not ever kill another human being without just cause, but the fury I experienced while I worked this job was more than I had ever felt. I didn't know what I would do. I was not impressed with this image of myself; it was not a pretty sight.

It was not until God showed me that a life was not mine

to take that I felt He'd helped me overcome those compulsions of the old man. I knew that instead of kill Taylor, I was to love him. And so while on my knees with clenched fists and gritted teeth and tears streaming down my cheeks, God got my promise. I could hate the sin but love the sinner. After our business was completed, God showed me where to find my killer.

I reasoned that I was looking for a man on the run, and that he was alone. If he acted true to form, he would have already killed Vonnie Stuth—if she was even the girl he mentioned in his letters. I began to put on his shoes, I began to be him. . . .

. . . *I have no money, and the license tags on my car are going to expire in six weeks. It would be stupid if I got picked up for the expired tags. I can't mail for the tags because there may be an APB on me and the police will be waiting at the address where the tags would be mailed. I'm going to have to pick them up in person . . . go to Michigan. Where do I get money for the trip? . . . Mom and Dad. They live in Tucson. They have always been supportive of me, and so has my wife. They know of some of my killings. I could call them collect and have them wire some money.*

I asked a friend of mine in Tucson to help me track down any communication between Taylor and his parents. I got access to phone records placing Taylor in numerous locales throughout the Southwest from which he made collect calls to the folks. His path was traced from Seattle cross country to Michigan, south to Louisiana, then Houston.

One morning soon after, I heard on the radio that a busload of schoolgirls were sniped at with a .22 caliber rifle in the Houston area. That was Taylor's M.O. (modus operandi, or method of operation); I knew it was him.

I contacted a friend of mine at the King County police department who was working this investigation. He was a Christian friend, and I trusted his discretion in hearing my argument. I had to go easy because the commander of the major crimes unit and I suffered a fractured relationship. He was convinced I was set out to embarrass them with my findings.

My friend asked me how I knew for sure that Taylor was in Houston. I had to tell him to trust me and call the Houston police and alert them. Houston made a check of local motels for an automobile meeting the description of Taylor's vehicle with his Michigan tags.

Two hours later they found him and burst into the room where he lay on the bed sleeping. A young girl was fastened to the bed naked. He was arrested with no resistance. He confessed to the murder of the Vonnie Stuth and described how he had raped her repeatedly and finally shot her in the back of the head and the middle of the back. He told her to run for it.

Gary Addison Taylor confessed to raping and killing a woman in Houston. His wife, Helen Taylor, approached authorities in San Diego, where she was staying with friends, and reported that there were three bodies buried at their former homes in Michigan and Washington—one they knew was going to be that of Vonnie Stuth. Taylor was then charged and convicted with the murders of the two Toledo women in Michigan, and was convicted of the rape and murder of Vonnie Stuth.

He admitted to being a woman-hater and had an official record of assault that spanned his entire adult life. He said he dreamed of shooting at downhill skiers, but despite the disappearance of a number of young women in the area of Colorado ski resorts and his presence in Colorado at the time, he said he never saw his dream become reality.[5] Although his movements paralleled the reports of several women gone missing throughout western states, Taylor denied having killed more than those four women. Like Thomas Creech, though, perhaps he'd been present at other murders.

At Taylor's sentencing, the judge described the heinous acts he committed against Vonnie Stuth. With her parents sitting in the gallery, cringing with every word, he spoke of the breasts bitten off and the teeth marks all over her body, including her crotch area. Taylor got ninety years with no chance of parole. As the prisoner was led from court, chained hand and foot, he paused and stared at me as we passed in the aisle, almost face to face. Hate and death was imbedded in the lines of his face, and he mouthed a few unintelligible words to me.

Gary Addison Taylor moved regularly over the months he

committed his crimes, usually well-versed at the overnight
disappearing act. He had little difficulty obtaining employ-
ment, even though he had begun a pattern of often leaving a
job without notice.

Taylor's wife and parents were aware of his crimes. The
letters point to an openness between Taylor and Helen about
all of his perverse activities. His parents were the first place he
turned when looking for solace in his flight; they'd been there
before when he was charged with attacks on women near their
home in St. Petersburg, Florida, when Taylor was just eighteen
years old.[6] They were there again in his escape from trouble
in Washington and Michigan.

The words of Helen Taylor after she alerted police of the
Michigan and Washington murders reveal the purpose of the
secrecy that she believed was necessary. Her attorney told the
press that she waited until after Gary Addison Taylor was
jailed to report the information because "she was afraid he
would get back at her."[7] One of the letters I found at the
house in Enumclaw was from Helen Taylor to her husband. It
read: "Dear Gary, . . . I have to go in spite of the fact I still
love you. . . . 19 years is a long involvement. I just can't go
from one crisis to another anymore."

How could so much tragedy strike one human being and
then spill over to touch everyone he knows and loves, as well
as many more he'd never met? The primary answer has to be
a state of irreconcilation with God. The curses of Deuteronomy
27 and 28 strike society and individual man when God's covenant is broken and God's means of reconciliation—belief in
the saving atonement of His Son, Jesus Christ—are rejected.
"If you are not for Me, you are against Me," said Christ. The
leader of the cause against Christ is Satan, so it is safe to
assume that tragedy, including the devastation that surrounded
the life and movements of Gary Addison Taylor, increases
with the degree of influence Satan has over someone.

Michael Wendland, a reporter with the *Detroit News* at the
time of the Michigan missing women cases, came to Seattle
during our investigation and told me of his findings linking
Taylor to the occult. His reports came from people Taylor had
known in the military who recall his fascination with and

constant talk about an ancient Oriental superstition implementing decapitation of an opponent killed in battle, a practice it is said was evident in some areas of the fighting in
Vietnam. The belief stems from a concern that, if the head is
not severed and buried separately, the spirit of the dead will
haunt its killer.

As I stated previously, Taylor attended classes on the occult with Dr. Richard Miller at the University of Washington
and sat, very likely, in the same room with Ted Bundy and
Thomas Eugene Creech. Creech had directed police to the
house in Burien, Washington, where four girls were decapitated in the style of the Oriental practice and claimed that he
had seen Bundy at satanic rituals taking place there and at
other locations. Creech also had last been seen in Washington
in the neighborhood where Taylor and his slain neighbor
Vonnie Stuth lived.

Did Gary Addison Taylor participate in—and adopt for his
own belief—satanism? I don't know, but I do know what I saw
as the aftermath of his reign of terror. The teeth marks on his
victims' bodies were identical to markings made by known
satanist killers. The handcuffs and sexual perversions, the
dreams about killing people, the proclivity for violence and
graphic images which played out in all of his confessed crimes,
all put him in the same category, as far as the outward result-
ing evidence shows, as Bundy and Creech, who have both
been linked more directly with the occult.

An involvement in the occult could also explain the fear
Helen Taylor had in reporting her husband's activities. It is
possible that she was well aware of what would happen to
someone who turned him in, because perhaps in the past he
had participated in the murders of those who had talked too
much about the cult's acts. The name of the friend she was
staying with after she left Taylor was in the list of names found
at his home. It might be nothing more than speculation, but
it is possible one of Taylor's destinations was San Diego—to
settle the score with his wife.

I was relieved when this investigation was closed, and I
praised and thanked God for the success He'd had through
me. I will never forget the image I had of God's hands deftly

moving people and circumstances around so that He could
present to me just the information I needed to proceed on the
case. I had been kept clear of danger, protected from my
enemies. Chapters 27 and 28 in Deuteronomy refer not only
to curses, but also to blessings when we take seriously the
word of God and apply it to our lives. We exist for His glory.
("Therefore whether you eat or drink, or whatever you do, do
all to the glory of God" [1 Cor. 10:31].) His majesty is mani-
fested every time I obey Him. I knew I couldn't have completed the investigation if I'd not given myself over to Him in
obedience, even in the relinquishing of my anger and hatred.

Blessed is he who considers the poor: the Lord will deliver
him in time of trouble. The Lord will preserve him, and keep
him alive; and he will be blessed on the earth; you will not
deliver him to the will of his enemies (Ps. 41:1,2).

The Killings Begin Again

> The descent to hell is easy, and those who begin by worshipping power soon worship evil.—C.S. Lewis, *The Allegory of Love*

There were several hundred deaths nationwide between 1975, when Gary Addison Taylor was sent to prison, and 1979. I investigated a small percentage of those, enough to know that the connection between killing and satanism was strong and, unbelievably, growing stronger.

An interesting theory has been put forth by scholar and theologian Dr. Gary North. In his previously referenced book, *Unholy Spirits*, he maintains that incidents of occultism throughout recorded history occur in a detectable pattern. North's research and analysis shows that these periods of godlessness cycle in at the end of a major definable age, as well as break out in spurts when a significant change occurs within the civilization. He adds that "Western civilization has experienced several outbreaks of occultism in the past, but has always suppressed them. Therefore, it has survived and flourished."[1]

Dr. North argues that

whenever the fundamental religious and philosophical

presuppositions that have predominated during one era in history are abandoned, or at least become increasingly doubtful among the spiritual, moral, intellectual, and political leaders of that civilization, the result is predictable: *a transformation of that civilization.* Social and political revolutions follow religious and philosophical revolutions.[2] (emphasis in original)

In other words, ideas have consequences.

Four revolutions in Western civilization have been accompanied at the time of the changing of the guard by a surge in occult activity. These are: 1) the sweeping change over classical civilization brought on by the spread of Christianity in the first century; 2) the Platonic early Middle Ages overthrown by the Aristotelian later Middle Ages; 3) Roman Catholic civilization stunned by the first worldwide revolution—the Reformation—a period North notes was marked by Roman paganism during the Renaissance; and 4) the twentieth century love affair with rationalism and humanism, beginning with Darwin and burgeoning now into the New Age movement.[3]

What does this have to do with the work of a Christian private investigator? Plenty, if that work increasingly focuses on occult-related crime, as mine was in the late seventies, out of necessity since the leaders of this age were speedily abandoning the "fundamental religious and philosophical presuppositions." I knew that the bizarre scenes I was reviewing and the horrific stories I was hearing were all part of a pattern already noted by theologians—a pattern I myself began to refer to as a rise in spiritual warfare. Each case was one more battle in the war over the culture.

I was gaining more and more experience in the investigation of occult-related crimes, detecting more and more similarity among those that were definitely linked to satanic rituals. There was enough evidence, though, to prove that a significant amount of difference existed in the variables from case to case. Satan's ways are widespread and diverse, and Satanists and occultists practice their worship of him in equally diverse ways. I've never been convinced that this diversity discredits the claim that satanism was the motivating force. I believe the occult was the catalyst; the diversity is easily explained by, first, the inability of sinners to be consistent in anything, and second, the natural desire to personalize our beliefs. Unless the beliefs are traditional in nature and personalization is prohibited by the tenets of the faith, as in God's warning that we are not to add or detract from His word (Rev. 22:18-19), man can not help but be inclined to improve upon the routine. ·

More Killings Began in 1979

From 1979 to 1981, a series of bizarre and horrible murders occurred in and around Atlanta, Georgia. Fear took root in the hearts of people nationwide, but nothing like the fear in those who lived in Fulton, Cobb, and Dekalb counties. From my roost in Seattle, I kept up with the news to see what the latest developments were in Atlanta, like I do with any mass or serial murder case. I never know if I am going to be called in, and I want to be prepared if my services are requested.

The killings continued, peaking to the chilling height of twenty-eight young Atlanta blacks, and before too long, a young man was arrested on the James Jackson Parkway Bridge, which spans the Chattahoochie River. His name was Wayne Williams, he was twenty-three years old, and he was being held in the deaths of two of the missing black youths.

In any case of this magnitude and notoriety, a defense team must be established by the lead attorney, much like the prosecutor sets up his case and lines up his witnesses. Cases like this, full of twists and turns and complexity, need expert witnesses to consider all the facets of the alleged crime, the characters involved, the defendant, and the evidence. Further, where there are cases with a large number of witnesses, the need for more than one attorney arises to keep track of testimony and logistics.

This case had six attorneys with Al Binder of Jackson, Mississippi, in command. In second position was Jim Kitchens, also of Jackson. They called me in because of my background in investigating crimes related to satanism and the occult. I was put in charge of the carpet and fiber evidence—for the media's sake—and told to keep quiet about the satanism aspect, if there was one. Above all, they cautioned, don't talk to the press.

When I left Seattle, even though I had no firm idea how long I'd be gone, I made arrangements to be in the East awhile. I'd learned long ago that not only are investigations into occult-related serial murders lengthy, but a day of a trial is like a thousand years of an investigation.

With preparations taken care of, I knelt before the Lord in silence—I didn't know what to pray. I was not sure that it was his will that I take this case. I mean I knew that I would end up in Atlanta only because He had decreed it in His secret will (Deut. 29:29), as He decrees all of life. ("In Him also we have obtained an inheritance, being predestined according to the purpose of Him who works all things according to the counsel of His will" [Eph. 1:11].) But I struggled over the act of walking out the door and heading to Atlanta—would it be reflecting His revealed will, the word of God? Did He want me there? Should I go? I wondered.

Sometimes God's direction is left only in the revealed will which states clearly that He expects us to do our job the best we can, to His glory, and to love Him with all our heart, soul, mind, and strength. I couldn't go against His plan, anyway; so what was left was to make a decision based upon what I know God requires of all believers, and prayed that I be used by Him. Knowledge of His secret will is not my jurisdiction, my right. Knowledge of His revealed will is my responsibility. I felt like Gideon; I wanted a sign.

The song of Gideon came to mind (paraphrased): *It's me again, oh Lord, it's me again. I hate to be a pest, but I don't think that I can pass the test. Just when I think I'm going to win, the doubt rolls in. I'm sorry, Lord, I must confess, it's me again. . . .*

The sign did not come . . .

I waited.

Psalms 46:10 says "Be still, and know that I am God." I waited for the voice of my shepherd, my master. In marine corps boot camp, we were taught to listen for the voice of our drill instructor and obey his command only. To that end, we were tested constantly. After chow, the recruits would run out to the "grinder" (parade field) in front of the mess hall, get in platoon formation, and await our drill instructor. He would come out the back door, sneak a peak around the corner, and sound attention from about a hundred yards away. We could not see him, we could only hear his voice, and God help those who did not snap to rigid attention at that precise moment.

The point is, always be ready, know what you are listening for, and when you hear it, don't hesitate: snap to rigid attention. In boot camp, the price of disobedience was a few lumps on the melon. With God, the price is either life or death.

While I waited, I went over in my mind all the things that the Lord had shown me in this area. The good times, the bad, the dangerous, but most of all, he showed me the responsibility I had. God had not opened my spiritual eyes to sit back and let someone else do the work. I was trained by God, and for his glory, and I knew what to look for in these investigations. Although I did not hear an audible voice, I heard that sweet inner voice that can only come from God, the peace of God that passes all understand that Jesus talks about in John 14 which settles over those who have rested in the knowledge of His word. I knew this case would test all areas of my training. There would be good times, there would be times of sorrow, there would be times of extreme danger, but I knew that the Lord would "go before me."

The next day, I reported to the defense team at the Fulton County courthouse in Atlanta. Wayne Williams had been arrested and released. The prosecutor could not make up his mind about the charge, but finally, I believe, folded under pressure from the public and elsewhere and was forced to develop a case against Williams.

I met all the players, including Binder and Kitchens and Binder's right-hand man, Derwood Myers, an ex-Marine and ex-cop. We hit it off immediately. He'd called me before I decided to come in on the case and said, "You know, I really would like your help; it seems you know a lot about the subject that we're dealing with. Maybe there's nothing to it, but we've heard rumors of the possibility of satanism, and we'll leave that up to you. But I've got to tell you right now, we don't have any money to pay you." We always said that if a movie on the murders was ever made, we'd all take our compensation then. I don't think anyone ever got a dime.

I spent the next two days reviewing police files and case reports and also developing a rapport with the attorneys and the other investigators. I told them I would need to have access to Wayne Williams whenever I wanted to talk to him. I also wanted to talk to as many police officers as I could.

It took me about two weeks of running back and forth looking into every wrinkle in the fabric of Wayne Williams and the cases before I was able to come up with anything concrete. I could see there was something unusual going on in Atlanta and the surrounding counties. After drawing up a list of questions, I contacted the police officers who did the initial reports to ask them about their personal feelings, their intuition—not typical police procedure, but as I'd said before, hunches very often have a seed of veracity hidden deep within. I also had several questions for Wayne.

I recall very vividly my first confrontation with Wayne Williams. I'd met him already in the course of my two-week investigation. Up until now it had always been a tough-guy routine; now I wanted to see inside Wayne Williams. I asked him, "Wayne, do you know why you're here?"

"What do you mean?" he said, puzzled but still a tough guy. "Of course I know why I'm here. Do you mean here in this room?"

"No," I countered, "why you're in this predicament."

"Yeah, I've been charged with a couple of murders I didn't commit."

I shook my head. "No, that's not why you're here. You're here because of what you believe, not because of what you've been doing. It's because of what you believe."

"What are you talking about, man?"

"I'm talking about the group you belong to. You belong to the Rastafary, the Black Hebrews, the Rastafarians."

He peered at me and wondered how much I knew.

I went on. "I know you're involved with quite a number of people. I know a lot of other things too; I know that there are people in high positions around here, in the police department, too who are involved in these things. I know for a fact that there are one or two detectives on this task force who belong to this cult group."

Wayne's face still had a funny look on it. Undaunted, I kept plunging forward. "I know who they are, and if you want me to expound on it, I will, but you know it's true." He listened.

I spoke to him two more times that same day. After a couple more days, he finally broke down. For the first time, I saw a different Wayne Williams. No longer cocky and self-assured, he was crying, whimpering. He was in fear, actually in fear.

Through his tears and cries, he said, "You don't know what you're saying, man. These people don't play games. They'll kill you. You can't get out of this satanism thing; you can't get out of this group."

The use of fear as a manipulator, keeping all their secrets safe—I'd seen it many times before.

"Look, Wayne, that's what they would have you believe. That's what they've said for years and years. You're not the first one whom I've run across like this. I don't have all the answers in this, but God does. You need to call on Him and trust Him. I know that at one time you used to go to Sunday school; you used to believe in God because your parents are Christian people. I know that because I've talked to them, and I believe and trust them. I've learned to love them in just the short amount of time we've known one another."

I continued on that track: "You know, they don't have this coming. You shouldn't be doing this to them. You have been so wrapped up in your world. You wanted to be this producer of rock music so badly that you got involved with the wrong crowd. I know the people you're involved with." I gave him a list of names, and his eyes just about bugged out of his head. He suddenly became real interested in what I had to say.

"Before I go any further, Wayne, let me say this, I don't believe you killed Tommy Ray Payne or Nathanial Cater. I don't believe you killed them, but I do believe you dumped their bodies. I think it was your job to dump them."

Wayne shook his head, still disbelieving there was any way to escape his handlers.

"It's all a lie, Wayne, including the threats that prevent you from leaving them. It's a total falsehood. The way out is narrow, but one exists—it's through Christ. The Lord wants to change you right now; we don't have time to fool around. We don't have time to think about it. You can't tell yourself that maybe another time you'll do this. Believe me, you need to go to your knees right now." The tears began again, for both of us.

"Wayne, I know you're concerned about your family, but these people aren't as tough and strong as they think they are. Their power is limited by the power of the blood of the cross. That's where you need to go."

Wayne's tears flowed as he hugged me. "It's time we got on to doing things right in the eyes of God," I said. He finally admitted that I was right, and even offered that there were a few things that I hadn't touched on. He asked me for some time to think about it all before we talked again.

That night the defense team had its nightly meeting to discuss the trial, the day's activities, and what had been discovered during the day. Assignments were given to the most appropriate person for various new jobs. Al Binder and Jim Kitchens would then direct specific questions to each of us. The meeting would conclude with one of the attorneys asking if anyone had anything to add. I decided I would divulge my findings.

"Gentlemen," I said, "I have something to add. I believe that what we have here is a series of ritual killings. First let me say that although I do not believe Wayne killed the two he is charged with [Jimmy Ray Payne, Nathanial Cater], I think he may have dumped one or both of the bodies." There was total silence as all eyes glared at me.

"Also," I added, "I believe we are talking about an occult group of about one hundred or more. They are known as the Rastafarians, this from evidence that a few of the bodies have been found with artifacts showing Black Hebrew markings on them near by. I have also learned that there are at least two members of this group on the police task force. Now if you don't believe that and think I'm crazy, just say so, and I'll be on the first flight home." I added that I was a Christian and that I would not stand by and pretend that this was not happening.

Al Binder was looking at me with his glasses perched on the end of his nose, a big cigar in his mouth. This is it, I thought. I'll be heading home soon; Binder's not buying any of this. Well, it was a chance I had to take.

"This is the reason you all brought me down here," I added.

There was total silence for a long thirty seconds as Al Binder stood up, walked toward me while rolling his cigar slowly around in his mouth. His piercing eyes kept staring into mine with not so much as a blink.

"Now Mr. Dena," Binder said, "Is there anything else you would like to add?"

"Yes, there is," I said. I elaborated on my findings in the case reports that three of the victims had satanic symbols carved on their bodies with a knife. Also, witnesses from the case files had told me about police officers who were Satanists. I did not just take their word for it; I had it checked out and had proof positive. Several of the young victims knew each other, and Wayne had some kind of affiliation with them. I also confessed that the day before, I had gone to Wayne to confront him, and that he admitted to me that he was a Satanist.

"Son," Al said, in his slow southern drawl, "I'm Jewish, but my wife is a Christian, and I love her. I love you, too, 'cause you're a fine detective." He smiled and shook my hand. He stepped back and said, "I was wondering how long it would take you to find out whether there was any truth to these rumors."

That night the defense team began to grow a lot closer; we started moving together in unison. Jim Kitchens pulled me aside, shook my hand, and said, "Praise the Lord, I had a feeling you might be a believer. I sure am thankful you are on this team." We all started communicating in a different tone and a better perspective because we all agreed what it was we were fighting for and against. That was the turning point for all of us.

The judge who was named to hear the case was Judge Clarence Cooper, a black man who was a Christian; I could tell by his comments throughout the trial. The press speculated that his appointment was related to the fact that he, Wayne Williams, and the victims were all black. In the courtroom, the stenographers, two of them, approached me and introduced themselves as Christians. They seemed to want to strike up a friendship. I met their husbands, and enjoyed some good fellowship with them. I was coming to the conclusion that we were all on the same team, battling against the same evil.

Soon after my arrival, the defense team reversed their directive to me about speaking to the press and asked me to hint at the type of work that I do when talking with reporters. I invariably included in every interview, every press conference, that I was a Christian. Phone calls, messages, notes began pouring in from all over the Atlanta area. Pastor So and So from such and such church wanted me to come visit the church, perhaps speak on some issues related to the occult and the case. I was invited to a lot of different functions by Christians just because I stood up and made my profession of Christ in the newspaper, told the public why I was in Atlanta, and asked for prayers. In all the bad there was some good.

From the moment the atmosphere started to change for the better, I was told to sit through the entire trial and not miss a thing. The defense wanted me to get a feel for any others who might get on the stand who held the same beliefs as Wayne's.

The prosecution team was made up of six attorneys. Lewis Sleyton was the prosecutor, and his second-in-command was Jack Mallard, a well-known litigator who went for the jugular. There were two Christians on the prosecution. Wally Speed, now in private practice in Atlanta, stopped me shortly after I made my public profession of faith and shook my hand.

"God bless you, Sal. I want you to know something; we may be on opposite sides of the fence, but we're brothers in the Lord. I believe what you say is true. I think you've done your homework." We had dinner together, along with his family and other attorneys. Wally stressed with a smile, "I normally wouldn't do this, but I'm taking a chance because we are brothers in the Lord and we're both working for the cause of truth and justice. In that sense we are both working for the same team."

Never once did Wally Speed use anything against me or the defense which I'd said in confidence.

The trial was a real battle of experts. The prosecution was good, but the defense stole the show. Al Binder and Jim Kitchens were truly the suave, smooth, southern gentlemen to the end. Binder even brought in F. Lee Bailey to observe the proceedings, his presence creating a flurry of activity among the press and disrupting the pace. I was impressed with the caliber of men and women I'd been called to work with. Additionally, I have continued to count most of them among my friends to this day. I did make a mistake one evening at dinner when I announced that I was finally getting used to all the southern accents. I was politely reminded that I was in Atlanta, and that I was the one with the accent.

A lot of times in cases like this we might ask a suspect, or someone who has confessed to a murder, why they have committed this act. The expectation is some bizarre or complicated or unbelievable answer. I guess I was thinking the same thing in this case, but it was not so.

I asked Wayne why he had gotten involved in this group, how he had gotten involved, why was he doing these things? His answer was very quick, concise, and simple.

"You know, Sal, if you look and see, most of the people around who have money are people who are involved in music, the ones of those who are the wealthiest are involved in the occult or satanism. A producer friend got me into it; I went to a lot of meetings, and it became clear the kind of money he was turning. I knew that it was for me. It looked like a lot of fun, a little bizarre, but the more I got into it, the more and more dangerous it got, and the more they expected from me."

In the end, Williams only revealed the names of people involved in the group if I asked point-blank, like, is this person in the group, or that? I would run a scenario by him, and he would admit or deny it. I've interviewed a lot of people in my life, and I've gotten a feel for truth-tellers and liars. In my opinion, Wayne Williams was telling me the truth.

I learned how a person like Wayne could fall for the lures of the occult. He is a highly intelligent person and the kind most people probably wouldn't like—especially as he appeared toward the end of the trial: pompous, with a chip on his shoulder, self-centered. After I cut through all of that pretense, I decided he really was a good conversationalist, fun to talk to, quick-witted, knowledgeable, and generally hard-working. Except for the travesty of his desire to have an easy road through the music business, he could be characterized as a hard worker, often keeping at something around the clock. I can't defend the actions of the man, or the sinful ways which led him down the criminal path, but I did learn to appreciate the good qualities God graciously endowed on Wayne Williams.

Wayne's parents, Homer and Fay Williams, lived out of town, across the street from the Baptist church they attended. Both were retired school teachers who adored their son. I believe, however, that they suffered from the mistake of letting him have his way too often. At seven or eight years old he started a radio station in his garage. He usually merely demanded something, and his parents jumped and met his wishes. Eventually, he was running the household. He just got a little too big for his britches.

Homer and Fay Williams, and Fay's sister, all admitted to being aware of Wayne's activities in satanism. When I confronted them with what I knew, I expected them to rant and rave and send me on my way. Instead, they said they knew I would figure it out and pledged their support for him as flesh-and-blood. "We won't sell him down the river." He practiced his faith within his home, and they never challenged him. An Egyptian book of magic, the Book of the Dead, was found in the family library. It detailed a lot of the same things Wayne was following, and there were several bookmarks in the pages.

I have seen several accounts about the Atlanta child murders, but not one that correctly depicted the hysteria, and the need the authorities felt to find someone guilty. I do not belittle the work done by the police task force or the prosecutor's office, because they never ceased to behave as only professionals would. I do believe however that there was tremendous pressure on the prosecutor's office to file charges against Williams. The pressure came from the governor's office, who, it was said, had received pressure from as high up as the president and vice-president of the United States. Then Vice-President George Bush visited with Atlanta Mayor Maynard Jackson as an emissary from President Reagan.[4] All the nation was anxious to close the case.

In the past, there has always been an attempt by police departments to keep crimes like this under wraps so there wouldn't be a large amount of hysteria. In the last few years, it has opened up quite a bit. It's been somewhat of an embarrassment to the authorities to have someone come in from the private sector, like myself, with expertise and experience they are lacking. The Wayne Williams case demonstrated an early willingness to alert the public that the police were investigating all angles of the crimes, including the realm of the esoteric.

It didn't ease the hysteria, which got completely out of control. Vigilante committees carrying baseball bats were formed in the city, and people were running around like sheep without a shepherd. Once I'd made my statement to the press that I was an expert in satanism, the occult, and witchcraft, the fear rose to new heights. So did attention from another quarter: the cultists themselves.

City under Siege

There is no way of victory over falsehood but by truth.
To have victory over the devil as a liar, and over his lies,
the believer must be determined always to know the
truth about everything, in himself, in others, and around
him.—Mrs. Jessie Penn-Lewis, *War on the Saints*

Even before Wayne Williams was arrested, the F.B.I. knew
they were dealing with ritual murders committed by a satanic
cult group. The problem was that they had no solid evidence
against any one person or persons due to the nature of the
crimes. According to an ex-F.B.I. man, the bureau had always
denied that this kind of a crime even exists.

I had never questioned whether crimes like this were related to the occult, and I soon became more convinced than
ever that that element played a significant part in Wayne
Williams' life as my investigation into his crimes ensued.

When my rental car was tampered with, that made me
aware that my presence on the defense team was making a few
people very nervous. Parked at the hotel, it had had the front
wheel covers removed and all but two of the lug nuts taken
off; one was left on each of the front wheels. The wheel covers

were then replaced. I thankfully had a background in the automotive business and detected the wobbling the loose wheels caused, probably long before someone not so automotively inclined would have noticed it. My suspicions were confirmed when the rental agency took the car back to their shop and reported the missing lug nuts to me.

The incidents continued. One evening as I left my hotel, I noticed that a car followed me out of the parking garage with three men in it. I got on the freeway heading north, and soon the driver pulled up alongside of me. I glanced over and couldn't believe what I saw! The guy in the front passenger seat was pointing a gun at me! Right here on an Atlanta highway, they were going to try to eliminate the threat of my poking around into their nefarious business. They tried a couple of times to pull up even with me so they could get a shot off, but traffic and Spirit-controlled, clear-headed thinking prevented their success.

I got as far as Buckhead before they tried it again. I knew that the more cars and people I kept around me, the safer I would be. I weaved in and out of traffic, my speed well beyond the limit. I finally pulled into a popular shopping mall, trying to cause as much commotion as I possibly could. In their attempt to pull alongside me they hit a parked car and smashed their front end. I made my getaway and decided not to return to my motel that night.

The next day, I mentioned to the defense team that I believed I might have been followed the night before. From that point on, I was extremely cautious, but I continued to survey those involved in Williams' group. There were still too many unanswered questions. After the next incident, I half-expected the rental company to refuse to let me take another one of their vehicles.

This time when I got into the car, my foot went to the floor when I hit the brakes, fortunately before I'd even started to move the car. I got out and checked the ground and found brake fluid underneath the car. The rental agency picked this one up, too, and reported that the rear brake lines had been severed from the slave cylinders. Again, there was no damage, no harm done to me—a warning, though, was obvious.

The last encounter with these people was a clear signal I was beginning to get too close in my investigation. Remember that my official area of oversight was listed as "fibers and carpets." Our fiber expert, Dr. Randy Breese, from Kansas State University, and I went down to the Chattahoochie River to collect fiber samples. The city of Atlanta is the largest U.S. center for the manufacture of carpets; most residential carpets originate there. There are carpet mills up and down the Chattahoochie which dump water in the river. You can't get within ten miles of a carpet mill without picking up a few minuscule carpet fibers, which we hoped to collect on a large scale that day.

We would stretch a white sheet out in the flow of the river, praying for a good sampling of trilobal fibers. A trilobal fiber is made up of three strands, two wrapped in one direction and the third wrapped in the opposite direction around those. It was, in that time of carpet manufacturing, a rare fiber.

We spent two or three hours in the water, propping the sheet up with poles to maximize the expanse of the sheet. We gathered a good supply of fibers and delivered our collection to a lab. Dr. Breese himself did the analysis and found several that were of trilobal construction, approximately ten different types of trilobal fibers within the several hundred different types collected altogether.

Carpet fibers, along with dog hairs, played a significant part in the pre-arrest investigation of Wayne Williams. A number of the victims had been found with fibers and hairs on them that were alien to their home environment. The prosecution tried to find a conclusive match to the fibers found in the home of Wayne Williams. The prosecution team disagreed among themselves as to how much assistance such evidence could be in the State's case against Williams, and we decided to capitalize on that discord and prove that these fibers could be found anywhere. (After all this work, it turned out that the court refused to accept the findings because the tests had not been done by their own experts and they questioned the methodology.)

I dropped Dr. Breese off at the lab, and I drove back to my hotel. I parked my car in the garage, recognizing a growing sense of unease. Instead of walking through the lobby to the elevator, I went up the back staircase. The recent incidents involving my car and the attempts to follow me came to mind, and I felt uncomfortable. I was wearing jeans, a sweatshirt, and tennis shoes instead of my usual attire of a business suit.

When I got to my floor and opened the door onto the corridor, my adrenaline started to flow. I looked down the hallway and saw a black man standing in the door to my room. He glanced at me and turned to say something to someone in the room. I took a few steps down the hallway, endeavoring to avoid appearing to have noticed strange people in my room. I didn't want to turn around or even hesitate for fear it would draw their attention to me

I heard a voice from the room say, "No, that's not our guy. Our guy always wears a three-piece suit." As I passed the room, I slid my eyes to glance in and saw another black man going through my suitcase. My observation quickly surveyed the two individuals, and I detected that the guy at the door was holding a gun down the length of his leg, half hidden by his body. I caught the elevator at the other end of the corridor and headed for the parking lot. Moving the car into a position where I could keep an eye on all entrances to the lot—I knew they had to have parked their car there, I waited with hopes to follow them.

My visitors came out of the hotel in a big hurry, and I took down their license numbers as they drove away. I was tempted to take more than their numbers, quelling a compulsion to put them down, take their guns, and teach them some manners. Had I done that, though, I wouldn't have been able to follow them and trace their associations.

Just like back home in Seattle, they led me to others.

I heard that a ritual was scheduled to take place one night, so I arranged to follow some of my regulars there. I told Jim Kitchens I'd be going, but no one else knew. I made arrangements to have a night scope and some back-up. The area the occultists were operating in was close to Stone Mountain and was heavily wooded and quiet. This time I parked about one mile away and worked my way back through the wood, where I saw their cars turn in.

My job in the marine corps was as a forward observer. I would call in mortar fire using a map and compass. Night compass marches were a specialty of mine. As I moved through the bush, I relied heavily on the night scope because I knew there would be guards on the perimeters.

Skulking through the bush at night is an extremely slow process, particularly if you are trying to be as quiet as possible. After about two hours, I made it to where I could see two fires burning about two hundred yards in front of me. Finally, I noticed the first armed guard about one hundred yards or more ahead. I continued to close in until I saw another guard. Now I was able to determine their perimeter.

I saw several people sitting on the ground in a semi-circle. They were all wearing heavy coats. Before long, twelve people came from somewhere beyond and formed a circle, standing up; all were dressed in long animal skins with the heads still attached. No one had undergarments on. Once they were in position, another person came and entered the circle of twelve. The twelve sat on the ground, and I began to detect that there had been extensive drug use before the ceremony began. The night scope caught their faces in clear view, and I observed signs of chemical intoxication, and my guess was that it wasn't alcohol.

The person in the center was a sight to behold, a short, fat man with a large stomach, wearing a black animal skin with some white spots on it. Affixed to his head was an ugly goat's head with long horns. He also was wearing nothing under the animal skin. I wondered how those people could be out there with no undergarments on. They must not be feeling much of anything due to the drugs, I thought, including the cold.

I studied the fat man in the center and noticed he was wearing something on his feet which appeared to be boots with cloven hooves on the front. He spoke, keeping his voice in a monotone, and the twelve repeated everything he said. The sound was haunting; the chanting served no aesthetic purpose; it was obvious they were attempting to call upon another realm. After about fifteen minutes, each of the twelve began to get up, one by one, and went to the outer semi-circle. They selected one person from there and brought them to

join the others in the full circle. This continued until everyone
in the outer circle was taken to the inner circle.

The ceremony continued. The fat man spoke again while
the original twelve repeated his words. Everyone in the circle
had their hands on those they'd brought into the ring, touching all parts of their bodies. This went on one by one until all
the new recruits were initiated. Then, as I suspected would
happen next, the fat man watched as each of the twelve had
sex with their initiates. Once that was done, unbelievable even
to my eyes, having witnessed these kinds of rituals before, all
the people watched as the fat man had sex with an animal.

It was after 3 A.M. when I headed for the car.

From that point on, it was like guerilla warfare. I knew
who they were, and they knew who I was.

What I found out through that encounter was a wealth of
information, including getting a better handle on the individuals involved in the satanic worship in the area. Again, however,
Wayne Williams never offered assistance in determining who
was in the cult, just nodding or denying when I asked him
about specific individuals. I did identify the two visitors to my
hotel room through the lenses of my night scope.

An abundance of evidence had been gathered, so I ceased
my night–time tactics and concentrated more on the trial. All
went smoothly until Wayne took the stand.

Since the beginning of the trial, people would line up in
front of the courthouse as early as 4:30 A.M. to be guaranteed
a seat. It was a first-come, first-serve basis. I noticed as the
spectators came in that there was a man with a large medallion
around his neck. After close scrutiny I identified it as a pentagram. The female with him was wearing earrings that were
silver crosses, upside down. There was also a black man with
a satanic "s" carved into both of his cheeks (similar to a light-
ning bolt). I was not the least bit surprised when I saw one of
my hotel visitors come in and sit down. We stared at each
other for a long time.

I let them all know I knew who they were. I even went to
each member of the defense team and pointed the people out
to them, being obvious about my motions. I also had two of
the detectives follow them when they left, adding their license

numbers to my list. As we stared each other down, we all knew we were involved in spiritual battle of the first degree. Their presence in the courtroom was not to visit the defendant; I believe they were there to intimidate Wayne, as a warning.

Occult involvement is much more extensive in Seattle than in Atlanta, but Atlanta suffers more than most cities. I believe both are particularly active centers of satanism because both were once very active pagan grounds of worship for the Native Americans. Satanists and occultists rely upon the availability of the spirits to whom they appeal for power—that is the purpose of the blood-letting and sexual rituals, to enhance energy and power—so they tend to congregate in areas where they believe ancient spirits are still hanging around, like burial grounds or former sites of worship.

I had never worked on a case involving the Rastafarians before this time. Since they were similar to satanism and witchcraft in their beliefs, though, I could count on some consistency in their habits as well. That's why I was able to track them so easily.

Rastafarians are most well-known—and popular role models among young people for these characteristics—for their life-style, in particular a love of reggae music, vegetarian dietary rules, wearing their hair in dreadlocks (uncombed locks and beards), and the smoking of ganja, or marijuana. Theirs is a political and religious cause. As followers of Haile Selassie I, former emperor of Ethiopia (who was born Ras Tafari), they believe blacks to be the Israelites reincarnated—thus the name Black Hebrews—and Ras Tafari their Messiah and champion of the blacks. Having been subject to the evil imperialism of the whites for centuries, Rastafarians call all blacks to Africa for repatriation and redemption out of this divine punishment for their sins. Once in this land, their true home and heaven on earth, they will be the rulers of whites.[1]

As a movement, the followers of this doctrine have been working their way through several different unconnected leaders since its inception in the early twentieth century. Jamaica has served as the proving ground for a number of its leaders, including several European and American blacks who have emigrated there to indulge in the life-style and then return to the West as reggae musicians. Today, however, many self-proclaimed Rastafarians have rejected the "Back to Africa" aspects of the movement and seek out the mystical elements, the militant black empowerment thrusts, or the fleshly pursuits of the culture.

Obviously not all participants in Rastafarianism are involved in ritual worship or activities that utilize blood-letting or sexual perversion. Most followers are young Americans or Europeans who join the counterculture movement of the day, selecting Rastafarianism for its non-white, non-Western sounding reggae music; its proclivity for mysticism, using marijuana as a vehicle to achieve transcendent states; and the dingy, scruffy look of dreadlocks. Sounds an awful lot like the hippie movement of the sixties and seventies. Youth around the world are very much alike from generation to generation; and Satan's followers, whether it's witchcraft, satanism, or any other group, know that the way to a young person's heart is through sensual, fleshly indulgences.

However, just as in the cases of the dabbler and the self-styled worshipper, these early-stage Rastafarians are oblivious to the profound meaning hard-core Rastafarians apply to their sensual activities. As with all groups, beliefs and rituals alter a little from city to city and group to group; consistency does lie in that they are often based upon the charisma of a leader and how he wants to define this particular group. If the leader leans toward violent or criminal acts in his methods of worship, then Rastafarians, too, can cross the line from constitutionally protected, anti-Christian religious worship into heinous, horrendous, bizarre, twisted, murderous behavior.

To them this is not murder, however. It is expected of them, and it is what they want to do. There were several theories floating around in Atlanta as to why it was young blacks (mostly boys) being killed. One of the more likely speculations centers on the idea that every one of the children were distributing drugs as well as selling on a small scale. It could be that these kids were talking and letting out information. I like some aspects of that theory, especially in conjunction with my findings that a form of satanism was being practiced. It is not unheard of to find hard-core occult groups involved in illegal money-making ventures on the side, like gambling, drugs, or prostitution.

An investigation requested by the Congress of Racial Equality (C.O.R.E.) was conducted by a separate security and law enforcement agency, G. Kelly Associates. The interim report on their investigation was released in December, 1981, arriving at much the same conclusions as I. Upon researching the involvement of cults in the Atlanta crimes, they stated:

> The cult now began to incorporate ritualistic sex into its philosophy and activities. Many of these rites had heavy sado-masochistic aspects as is the case with similar cultic groups. The pragmatic problem of dealing with dishonest underlings afforded the group a means of eliminating these traitors and also satisfying the rituals demanded by their ideology.

> Cult dynamics aside, such deviate practices have a pattern of escalating until they become insatiable, and as in similar historic occurrences, these nepharious[*sic*] activities come to light when this insatiability creates a frequency of bizarre activities which attracts public attention.[2]

I am convinced this Black Hebrew sect was using young blacks in a form of sacrifice. Obstacles continued to impede my investigation, this time in the pursuit of evidence pointing to the mutilation of the victims. Most of the victims had been killed by strangulation, a popular ritualistic method. A few of the victims had knife wounds, indicating that they had perhaps struggled or tried to escape. I'd heard that some of the children's bodies were carved up with satanic symbols. When I tried to get reports about this from the police departments, they were not available to me. We forced them from the prosecution through discovery, then found that none of the records had any evidence of such markings. I continued to dig. Some good people in a couple of the police departments slipped me a file here and there, setting off an uproar among the authorities and the prosecutor's office. The rumors had been correct.

The jury found Wayne Williams guilty on two counts of

murder. He did not divulge any information on the group, but
instead went to prison out of fear of retaliation. Within minutes of Wayne's guilty verdict, T-shirts went on sale in the
courthouse. One shirt, green in color, the same shade as
Wayne's carpet at home, read "This T-shirt made from the
fibers of Wayne Williams' carpet." Another shirt, in black,
read "Wayne Williams leaves you breathless."

I was never able to prove any connection between the
satanic activity in Atlanta, the Black Hebrew group of which
Wayne Williams admitted being a part, and the deaths of the
children, including the two whose deaths brought about
Wayne's conviction. My investigation, however, did uncover
enough material to allow for speculation, and while speculation is not sufficient to convict someone, it does provide evidence of a need for revival in a city. Atlanta was in trouble.

According to a March 1982 addendum to the G. Kelly
Associates December 1981 interim report, one of the witnesses called by the defense team on behalf of Wayne Williams admitted later that she had lied on the stand to protect
Williams.

> She admits that she intentionally and systematically kept
> from her testimony knowledge of Williams' involvement
> in satanic rituals. She alleges that Williams invited her
> to attend and participate in witchcraft and sacrificial
> ceremonies. Additionally, she claims that Williams told
> her that he believed he had been reincarnated several
> times and that during one of his previous incarnations
> was present in the Ford Theatre during Lincoln's assas-
> sination.[3]

After the fact, an article appeared in *US* magazine (30
March 1982) featuring the "eyewitness" account of Shirley
McGill, a Miami woman I also interviewed as an associate of
the cult. As the bookkeeper for a drug dealer, she followed
her boss to Atlanta to take care of some business there and
met some people with some very bizarre habits. Her claim
centered on the methods of killing used by the cult. She told
US magazine:

> I was doing the books one day when this child came in.
> Two men had him, one on each arm, and my boyfriend

was behind them. The child was crying. He looked at me and said, "Help me, please. They're going to hurt me." I said, "They're not going to hurt you." I didn't think they would. They took him out into the bedroom and about 15 minutes later they came out. I looked around and said, "Where's the child?" I went into the bedroom and they had him tied. His hands were behind his back and he was on his knees and his legs were tied. And water was just running out of his eyes, he was crying so. I walked over and there was a plastic bag in his mouth. I could see it sticking out of his mouth. He was choking. I tried to pull it out, but just as I did, he died.[4]

Williams, McGill confirmed, did not kill anyone. She identified him as a member of the cult, whose role was to seek out sacrifices, take pornographic pictures, and dump the bodies. She also believes the killings fell into two categories: sacrifice and murder, the latter being reserved for those drug runners who talked too much. McGill went public with her fears and her testimony after a friend, who posed for pornographic pictures for the cult and began stealing from the group to support a drug habit, was found murdered, surrounded by satanic symbols.[5]

Attempts to discredit her story ran just as fast through the media wires as the gory details themselves did. Her name was leaked, and immediately she was labelled a prostitute and alleged murderer. Even though Shirley McGill passed lie detector tests and psychiatric evaluation, and some of the victims *had* been killed by having a plastic bag placed over their heads or down their throats, and Wayne Williams admitted to being involved in satanic activity, and I myself witnessed occult rituals, none of this was enough to bring any convictions against anyone other than Wayne Williams. He, after all, had been the last one seen with the bodies of Nathanial Cater and Jimmy Ray Payne. He had been the one to dump them into the Chattahoochie River.

One of the theories to come out of follow-up investigation of this case includes an association between the satanic activities taking place in Atlanta and the Son of Sam case in New

York. David Berkowitz, the serial killer charged in the 1979
Son of Sam murders, "has stated absolutely that the Son of
Sam killings were ritualistic practices of a satanic group. He
claims that the group is a loosely-knit national organization."[6]
His statements include references to a peripheral sect of the
Church of Scientology:

> Berkowitz, in a recent deposition, seems to be alluding
> to an organization known as "The Process," which is a
> splinter group from the more well known Church of
> Scientology. The Process is known to be a violence-
> oriented, ritualistic satanic cult. Among the more no-
> table Process groups, or spin-off groups, is Charles
> Manson's "family". It is interesting to note that one of
> the terms Shirley McGill uses for the devil, or the indi-
> vidual leading the rituals she attended in Atlanta, is the
> "Creepy Crawler" which is a name Manson liked to use.

> There appears to be a growing relationship between
> Williams' group in Atlanta and Berkowitz's satanic group
> in and around New York City.[7]

What role did Wayne Williams play? He admitted to me
that it was his job to pick up young children and then to
dispose of their bodies off the James Jackson Parkway Bridge.
I suspect that he had this assignment because he had a lot of
contact with young people. He would put ads in the paper
looking for boys who wanted to be a rock-and-roll star or in
the movies. "I'll see what your talent is and what we can do to
get you under the lights," he'd promise. Cater and Payne were
older, in their twenties, not the typical sacrifice victim, and
they were addicted to drugs. I believe they were likely murdered to keep them quiet.

To this day, I am convinced that Wayne Williams is inno-
cent of murder, but guilty of worshipping Satan. I'll never
forget the look he gave me when I told him that he had found
himself in prison not because of anything he had done, but
because of what he believed. It's a lesson to all of us, especially
non-believers, whether they are worshippers of Satan or not.
God doesn't send sin to hell; He sends sinners. Our actions
betray our hearts. Those who hate God will be destroyed; read
the prophets if you don't believe me.

A Spy Manual:
Orders from Headquarters

> Prayer is request. The essence of request, as distinct from compulsion, is that it may or may not be granted. And if an infinitely wise Being listens to the requests of finite and foolish creatures, of course He will sometimes grant and sometimes refuse them.—C.S. Lewis, "The Efficacy of Prayer," *The World's Last Night and Other Essays*, (1959)

Everything needs a plan. There are blueprints for building a house, diagrams for a car, an outline for a book, instructions for a tricycle, and the Word of God for our lives. What happens if you don't follow a plan? Well, I think it's safe to say you'll end up with more than a few nuts and bolts left over.

God is not the God of chaos; the whole universe is a creation of related parts. Man himself is an awesome machine. Can we know everything there is to know about the universe or man? We don't yet; in fact, we don't even know everything that we have yet to know. We also don't know whether God will reveal all the workings of creation or man. It is His prerogative as Creator to determine what He will reveal about us. This is a special liberty creators have. When you discover a unique way to roast a chicken, do you write up everything you thought and did in the process when you send the recipe in to a magazine? No, it's your prerogative to include only what you determine is necessary for others to follow and roast the chicken the way you planned.

God knows what it is we need to know in order to follow His plan for our lives, only what He has determined is enough. Just as He promised never to burden us beyond our ability to withstand the trials, we can trust His character to be the same when it comes to the knowledge of Him. He will never hold us accountable for more than He has revealed to us.

This does not mean we cannot know God fully. In a sense, in the way we as the creation are able, we can have a full understanding of our Creator. As His image, His reflection, we know that we have more than just part of Him in our soul, God's sustaining hand transmutes some of His characteristics to us. When we are converted and adopted into His family, our awareness of His evidences in creation and in our lives are sharpened even more.

But we must understand that not everything is knowable. God has His secret will, and He says that the secret things *belong to Him* (Deut. 29:29). This means that His determinations—His decrees—that He has not revealed to us are not ours; we have no claim, no rights, no jurisdiction. This can be carried further to say that when we venture into questions about God's plan, His ways, or His characteristics which cannot be settled by looking into His revealed will—creation and the Word—then we are trespassing onto His territory. Providence belongs to Him. As children, someday we will know. No parent, though, answers in full every query of his children.

When I do the work of a private investigator who is bound to the ways of the Lord, I follow the plan of God that has been made available to me. I don't know everything, but I know enough. And God promises to make His wisdom available to me as I need it. I am reminded often of the story in I Kings of Solomon and the two women who both claimed to be the mother of a living child.

Now two women . . . came to the king and stood before him. And one woman said, "O my lord, this woman and I dwell in the same house; and I gave birth while she was in the house. Then it happened, the third day after I had given birth, that this woman also gave birth. And we were together; no one was with us in the house, except the two of us in the house. And this woman's son died in the night, because she lay on him. So she arose in the middle of the night and took my son from my side, while your maidservant slept, and laid him in her bosom, and laid her dead child in my bosom. And when I rose in the morning to nurse my son, there he was, dead. But when I had examined him in the morning, indeed, he was not my son whom I had borne."

Then the other woman said, "No! But the living one is my son, and the dead one is your son." And the first woman said, "No! But the dead one is your son, and the living one is my son." Thus they spoke before the king.

And the king said, "The one says, 'This is my son, who lives, and your son is the dead one'; and the other says, 'No! But your son is the dead one, and my son is the living one.'" Then the king said, "Bring me a sword." So they brought a sword before the king. And the king said, "Divide the living child in two, and give half to one, and half to the other."

Then the woman whose son was living spoke to the king, for she yearned with compassion for her son; and she said, "O my lord, give her the living child, and by no means kill him!" But the other said, "Let him be neither mine nor yours, but divide him."

So the king answered and said, "Give the first woman the living child, and by no means kill him; she is his mother."

And all Israel heard of the judgment which the king had rendered; and they feared the king, for they saw that the wisdom of God was in him to administer justice. (I Kings 3:15-28)

This is wisdom at work, and it is a wisdom available to us, evidenced by its appearance in the Bible, again the revealed will of God. Solomon reflected the image of God in no more enhanced or transcendent way than any other human. God simply helped him use his measure of wisdom in productive, visible ways for the manifestation of His own glory. Solomon may have been used specifically for a purpose and given the wisdom he needed to complete his task, a wisdom that possibly is unavailable to anyone else. He would thereby differ from us in that respect. *But we don't know that.* We do know that his wisdom (endowed by God) was set up as a standard for us all.

From the moment I was transferred from the kingdom of darkness into the kingdom of Jesus Christ, I was challenged to work out many cases with all the wisdom I could muster. Most of it came from the word of God—the rest was thanks to His hand resting on me.

While I was in the midst of the Gary Addison Taylor and Ted Bundy investigations, I received a call from the parents of a sixteen-year-old girl who had been missing for about two months. She lived less than one-half mile from Taylor's house by the airport. Her parents had been told by the police department that there were no fresh leads, so not a whole lot was being done. Rumors were circulating among the King County police that this girl had been used in a ritual killing and that she had been strung up by her heels, her throat had been cut, and the blood had been consumed.

From the beginning, I didn't believe the story, because that's just not how a ritual is performed. All rituals had purpose to them, and I couldn't detect from my investigation that there was any reason for the local occult groups to sacrifice this girl or involve her in any of their rituals. Additionally, the groups that perform those rituals don't go around announcing what they do; they try to remain secretive. "Occult," remember, means hidden.

I strongly felt that Marilyn Maxine Straight, the missing girl, was not a member or a sacrifice of a cult. The only other way she could have been killed the way the rumor claimed she was was for her to have infiltrated the cult, without being committed to its beliefs and activities, for some reason. Not only is it not likely for a sixteen-year-old girl to do such a thing, one of the most difficult feats in this business is to assimilate into a ritual of this kind. It's possible, and extremely dangerous, and therefore I could not place her disappearance in that category.

I met with the parents to discuss their daughter's background: the things she liked to do, places she liked to go. They reassured me that she was not the type to run away and that she had every reason to want to stay. They decided to hire me and inquired about my fee. I could see that this was a family of little means; to try and scrape up any amount of money would be next to impossible.

The mother looked at me with tears in her eyes and said, "I guess it's only rich people who can afford to have their children found. I'm sorry, we can't afford you." The father sat hanging his head, holding a small paper bag with money in it; I knew because I could hear the coins rattling.

At that very moment, the Lord touched my heart and put words into my mouth. "How much do you have there?" I asked. With his eyes shining with tears and a look of anticipation on his face, he blurted out, "Fifty dollars."

"That just happens to be today's discounted price," I said. I would have done it for no fee, but I didn't want to injure their pride or self-respect. I took the bag home and put it in my desk; I didn't even look into it.

I went to Marilyn's school and talked to her teachers and some of her friends. I started putting together a picture of a young girl who lived a life of embarrassment, who was teased repeatedly by her peers because she couldn't afford to wear the designer brand jeans and the fancy new tennis shoes all the others wore. I recalled seeing where she slept at home; it was not a room but a little cubby hole with boxes to keep her clothes in.

The thoughts of my childhood raced through my mind as I remembered that I had grown up the very same way, but with a large family. I too was teased because my parents could not afford to dress me like everyone else. I was also teased for what I would have in my lunch bag. I come from a large

Mexican-American family, and there wasn't always enough money to buy bread for sandwiches. My mother would pack us tortillas with beans, and that always drew ridicule and derision.

Young kids can be so mean and heartless. Boy, could I identify with this girl. As I grew older, I began to fight back, and all the teasing stopped. Today, at six feet and two-hundred pounds, an ex-marine with a black belt in karate, few have the guts to tease me. The Lord found a way for me to escape, but this girl had no escape. I will never turn my back on the poor; nor will I ever forget where I came from.

This was such a common problem for me to encounter: young people gone missing because of feelings of low self-worth and inadequacy. Steve Russo of Steve Russo Evangelistic Team, a youth evangelism project in southern California, has told me that he believes those kids who are most vulnerable to being lured into the cult are runaways, abandoned, directionless kids. Just because a kid doesn't fall into one of these categories right now doesn't mean he may not be there at some time. The way to protect a child from the occult is to protect them from the perimeter of the occult. Russo's belief is that the best method to accomplish this is for parents to "assure kids of your unconditional love."[1]

I can't say whether Marilyn Maxine Straight recognized the feelings of devotion and protection her parents held for her, but somewhere the communication broke down. She was gone, and here I was, hired for the purpose of trying to find her, praying she hadn't gone from the sphere of the family to the sphere of the runaways to the sphere of the occult.

By this time I had worn out a considerable amount of shoe leather, so it was about time for me to go to my knees. I was using my access to the tool of prayer to balance the use of the tools God had given me to investigate this case. God, being the tool-maker, had the plan firmly in His mind; I was trying to decipher the instructions.

"Father," I prayed, "You know me, you know when I sit and when I rise . . . Lord, you groomed me for this job, You put me in touch with this family for a purpose. If it be Thy will, show me what to do, where to look, and I promise I will do my best for this family and for Your glory."

The next day, I stopped by the home of the parents to bring them up to speed on what I had been doing. As I covered my steps over the past day or two, the mother kept yawning. She apologized and explained that she hadn't gotten much sleep the night before. For the last two weeks, she added, the phone would ring well after midnight, and when they would answer, the party on the other end would say nothing. This had happened four times in two weeks. Last night's call was a little different in that the party on the other end seemed to be crying very softly.

I knew then that I was close to the end of the investigation. I told them that I felt it might be their daughter calling, and that out of loneliness or homesickness she probably just wanted to hear their voices.

"Look," I said, "We have nothing to lose. The next time you get a call like that, I want you to believe it's her and talk to her. Tell her you love her and that you miss her, and to please come home." I gave them some ideas. "Tell her, 'If you need money, we will send it, and above all, if you have done anything wrong, forget it, all is forgiven. We just want you to come home because we love you.'"

They agreed to try it. I had both parents practice the speech, and after a few days, I made a pretend call to their home to see if they were doing it correctly. They passed the test with flying colors and recited their speech like parrots. They were ready to help me bring their daughter home.

The next day, about 2 A.M., the call came; the mother did her job, and the voice on the other end began crying. Marilyn said, "Oh Mom, I love you too, and I want to come home, but I don't think these two guys will let me go."

The mother got the address in Portland, Oregon, and told her daughter that a friend would be there shortly. Three hours later I pulled into the driveway in Portland and noticed a young lady through the window, a dim light shining behind her. She opened the door quietly and whispered my name. She pointed to the darkened back rooms and warned me that we might be heard. Sure enough, a young man appeared in jeans and an older man behind him. They asked what I was doing there and ordered me to leave. Time for a personality change.

I pulled my automatic out of my belt and pushed it in their faces. "Shut up and pick up those boxes and put them in my car; I'm giving the orders now," I barked. In a few minutes, Marilyn and I were on I-5 heading north to Seattle. Her rescue had been amazingly easy.

My first question to her was "Have you any idea how much your parents love you?" She began to cry, and the tears continued to flow for most of the drive home. I told her about her parents' love for her, but more importantly, I told her about God's love for her.

Some old habits are hard to break, or maybe it was the marine in me, but eventually, I began to debrief her. Why did she go? How did she survive? What made her contact her parents?

She left because she was pregnant and didn't want to be hassled by her peers anymore. (And the pro-abortion forces say the most dangerous—and frightening—element in a pregnant teen's life is her parents! They've forgotten how cruel "friends" can be. Perhaps if they'd allow states to institute at the very least parental notification if not parental permission laws, there would be someone to help protect a young, pregnant girl from the unkindnesses of peers.)

Marilyn told me she hitchhiked to Portland and met a young man who took her in and became her lover. When he found out she was pregnant, he just assumed that he was the father. They decided immediately that she would have an abortion. After she had aborted the child, she became homesick and wanted to return to Seattle. The boy's father didn't want her to go for fear she would tell her parents about the abortion and they would hold him accountable as the responsible adult.

She wouldn't talk when she called because she was afraid to even discuss the pregnancy or abortion with her parents. All she could do was cry, not realizing that they were the ones who could best shelter and comfort her.

She was right in a sense; her parents would not have understood at the time. That was one of the first questions I had asked them. Their answer was "Absolutely not; no way." They didn't even want to discuss the possibility of her being pregnant. But they learned that the pain of not knowing whether she was alive and safe far surpassed the pain that the discovery of her pregnancy might have caused.

It's been said that time heals all wounds. In this case, God did indeed use time and, in His infinite wisdom, a short separation. I took her home and waited around long enough for her to tell her story and have her parents forgive her. While the tears were flowing, I slipped out the door and headed for home. Once there, I plopped down at my desk. It had been a long night, and I needed sleep. But first, I wanted to unwind for a few minutes. It always feels good to bring an investigation to a close, especially when I can help reunite a family.

Thinking of this and checking up on my work-to-do, I opened the lower desk drawer and saw the paper bag with the fifty dollars in it. I pulled it out and emptied it on the desk. There was one ten-dollar bill, two fives, eleven ones, and the rest in change. They had literally broken the piggy bank.

> He who dwells in the secret place of the Most High shall abide under the shadow of the Almighty . . . He is my refuge and my fortress: My God, in Him will I trust . . . For he shall give His angels charge over you, to keep you in all your ways . . . Because he has set his love upon me, therefore I will deliver him: I will set him on high, because he has known My name. He shall call upon Me, and I will answer him; I will be with him in trouble; I will deliver him and honor him. (Psalms 91:1-2,11,14-15)

God's ways of bringing about His will often include our mistakes and the lessons learned from them.

The number of participants in the house was thirteen, the correct number to make up the "council of the thirteen" (to coincide with Christ and his twelve disciples). They were followers of Richard Miller, the Seattle witch who taught parapsychology classes at the University of Washington, in which sat Ted Bundy, Thomas Creech, and Gary Taylor. I regularly followed the thirteen to learn more about them, this time tracking a husband and wife to this split-level home. The rear door to the basement was open, though locked. I followed sounds of chanting up the stairs to a point of observation.

All the members had hooded robes on. The leader wore a white robe, while the rest were in black. All the garments were slit up the sides to just under the arms, and no one wore underclothes, so I knew that I was about to witness an orgy.

All of a sudden—and I don't know how it happened—I was spotted. I jumped from my hiding place and ran to my car as fast as I could. The members had to remove their robes and put pants on in order to chase me, I presume because they didn't want to chance being seen in their gowns. Thank God for small favors!

I got to my car about the time seven or eight members were exiting the house. I was so scared I couldn't even get the key into the ignition. When I finally did, I revved the car up and put it in gear so fast that the tires squealed and the car jerked into motion. Once on the road, it only took a minute or two for me to realize that this had all occurred through my own stupidity and not waiting on the Lord. Never again did I attempt to go ahead of God, without his approval, and on my own power. Had I not made a clean break . . . I shudder to think of the possible outcome; I could have been used as a sacrifice in a sexual ritualistic orgy.

What does light have to do with darkness? the apostle questions, What does a Christian have to do with evil? I was new in this type of investigation and immature in the Lord. With God's grace and providence I got out of there.

> Then said I, Ah, Lord God! behold, I cannot speak: for I am a child. But the Lord said unto me, Say not I am a child; for thou shalt go to all that I shall send thee, and whosoever I command thee thou shall speak. Be not afraid of their faces; for I am with thee to deliver thee, saith the Lord. Then the Lord put forth his hand, and touched my mouth. And the Lord said unto to me, behold, I have put my words in thy mouth. (Jer. 1:6)

I still didn't do everything within the revealed will of God. I was still learning this new game.

One day I visited the occult bookstore belonging to Richard Miller. I walked in and made my way to the book racks and knelt down to inspect them more closely. I had noticed about six people in the store and saw Miller in the corner talking to someone, his back to me.

A few moments later, I heard a deep voice announce, "There's a Christian in here; I can feel him." I could hear Miller's footsteps as he walked toward me on the wooden floor. He rounded the corner, pointed at me, and said, "And there he is." I very calmly stood up and explained that I was looking for a particular book, which I was. I was trying to put together a calendar of their holidays and had decided to go straight to the source. In retrospect, it was a foolish move on my part, and I would never do it again. Thoughts of Christ's confrontation with Satan on the mountain top came to me, and I realized I should not have put God to such a foolish test.

As you probably may have guessed, Miller asked me to leave, and to this day, I wonder what he would have done had I tried to witness to him.

As Christian believers, we have all come across divisions in our churches where the pastor doesn't agree with the deacon board or vice versa, or the steering committee is going in the wrong direction, or no one in the choir can agree on the color or the style of the new robes. And the list goes on and on and on. Come on, people, where do you think the strife is coming from? Satan!

There is nothing more exhausting than doing spiritual battle with Satan. God never promised following His plan would be easy, only simple. With all the references to running races and servitude, I don't believe God meant the Christian walk to be a stroll in the park. My experiences tend to be more along the lines of a foray into the jungle.

A lot needed to be learned, and as late as 1982, I was still getting instruction from the Lord on how to be a good detective. I was asked to speak on satanism and witchcraft at a local college shortly after I returned from investigating the child murders in Atlanta. A large crowd responded to the local newspaper advertisements, and notices on campus invited the whole campus and community to come hear about the Ted Bundy killings and the Atlanta murders.

After I accepted the speaking engagement, I sat down and thought about what I was doing. For the first time, I would be speaking to a secular group, on a college campus, about a subject that was highly controversial. There was a good chance opposition from the other camp would show up. The thought was harrowing. I did then what I should have done even before I accepted the invitation; I went to my knees and humbled myself before the Lord.

"Father, this is your show, and I know I'm just your messenger. If it be Thy will and if this is Your time, use me to say what You want those people to hear."

I went to bed that night and slept like a baby. I felt not a care. The next day I arrived at the college and was informed that I was to fill a five-hour time frame in order to address as many people as possible.

Theoretically, the coordinator informed me, the students would be in and out since classes met every hour. I was also told that I could expect vocal opposition. I folded up my notes and put them away after seeing the hecklers. It was clear a whole different agenda was going to be attempted here, and I concurred that God's methods would be a much more effective approach than my own. I realized that, deep down, I knew all I had to do was show up and the Lord would do the rest.

I laid the groundwork for the day with a word of testimony. "I am here because I am a born-again Christian believer," I heard myself say. "I know that there are those here today who believe in Satan or are involved in some kind of occult group. Are you man or woman enough to admit it?" I challenged. "Come on," I said, "I admit where I stand; you do the same."

Three hands went up, two guys and a girl. The eyes of all the spectators moved back and forth like they were at a tennis match; first at them, then at me. "I rebuke you and bind you in the name of Jesus Christ," I said in a firm and loud voice that brought total silence to the field of battle.

"Now then," I said in a softer and kinder voice, "Through the power of Christ, I render you speechless and helpless as we discuss this topic today." The two guys walked out with their heads bowed, one after the other, like puppies that had been swatted with a newspaper. The girl remained and looked me straight in the eye. "Young lady," I said. "Since you won't be able to talk, I want you to help me. If I lie or distort the truth in any way, I want you to jump up and wave your arms, but if I tell the truth, I want you to shake your head up and down in agreement, Okay?" She nodded her head. No one else dared to heckle or even cause a commotion for five hours.

Have you ever noticed a dog on the street? When he's by himself, he's just fine. When you get two or three together, they are emboldened. When you get a half dozen together, you have a mob; they run over everything and create as much chaos as possible. That's what those hecklers were like. You need to hit fast and hard to take the wind out of their sails, and that is what the Lord did that day in front of several witnesses. He is the one who can calm the angry seas with just the wave of His hand.

When it was over, about fifty Christians gathered around the podium to greet me. We thanked God for doing battle and giving us victory that day. I have found that when we acknowledge our weaknesses to God like Jehosephat did, the Lord is willing, able, and even delighted to bear our burdens. Jehosephat prayed, "Lord, we have no power or might against our enemy, so our eyes are on you." God cleared that battlefield of wild dogs in a real hurry.

> And every spirit that does not confess that Jesus Christ
> has come in the flesh is not of God; and this is the spirit
> of the Antichrist, which you have heard was coming,
> and is now already in the world. (I John 4:3)

Never underestimate your enemy. I have crossed paths with those who have power from the other side who will try to infiltrate the body of Christ. The Bible calls them "the fierce wolves of the pack." They will come and try to deceive the very elect. We must realize that "not all spirits are of God," we must "test the spirits," we must gain discernment through the word and meditate on scripture. And having done that, "put on the full armor of God, so that you will be able to withstand the wiles of the devil." No one has the power that the Christian has in thwarting the devil.

To some people, those words of warfare are just interesting reading from the sixth chapter of Ephesians. The Bible says that Satan is constantly on the prowl, "seeking whom he may devour." He has been known to make his own plans to capture and destroy. Thankfully his plans are never absolute. I am cautious to give credence to the warnings of those who believe that Satan's demons are under every rock or behind every bush. This simply is not true; let's not give Satan too much credit. He is not like God, and he cannot be every place at once. Only God is omnipresent and omnipotent.

The Lord is on our side, and He's given us all the directions we need to live eternally.

My Pain, His Gain

God, who foresaw your tribulation, has specifically armed you to go through it, not without pain but without stain . . . —C.S. Lewis, *Letters of C.S. Lewis* (2 September 1949)

Have you not known? Have you not heard? The everlasting God, the Lord, the Creator of the ends of the earth, neither faints nor is weary. His understanding is unsearchable. He gives power to the weak, and to those who have no might He increases strength. Even the youths shall faint and be weary, and the young men shall utterly fall, but those who wait on the Lord shall renew their strength; they shall mount up with wings like eagles, they shall run and not be weary, they shall walk and not faint. (Isa. 40:28-31)

The year 1978 brought with it a much needed time of personal renewal. Even though the killings were just beginning in Atlanta, there was no case at the time, and no one had heard of Wayne Williams. But since the close of the Gary Addison Taylor case, my reputation had already begun to build, and I was into an entirely new phase of my career. For

over three years, I was stuck in high gear and couldn't find a
way to slow down, but God could. I had been so busy with all
the investigations, travel, speaking engagements, deprogrammings, and study. If that weren't enough, we owned two auto
body shops, a shopping center, a beauty salon, and I was the
vice-president of a Christian counseling center. You can only
keep a bow bent so long. Sooner or later, something has to
give.

Through my own stupidity, I developed difficulties with
the IRS in one of my businesses and problems with cash flow
in another. My marriage was suffering, and it was no wonder
I had a bad case of stress. It was so bad, I couldn't even go to
work. I was literally "on the couch" for about six months. The
most mundane decision had to be made first thing in the
morning, because I was too exhausted by noon to think straight.

For three years I had been identifying and working with
satanic attacks on others, but when it happened to me, I
couldn't see it. I was paranoid, physically weak, and fearful of
the dark. Some well-intentioned friends came to me with advice. "You need to think positive," one said and handed me a
book. Another said, "You need exercise and fresh air." A third
one said that I should go have a few drinks and kick up my
heels. I was reminded of Job and his friends, though I was
hardly the righteous and upright servant that Job had been. It
was sometime later that I realized that these friends were
"physicians of no value."

One day my wife came and sat down next to me and said,
"Sal, the Bible says that God will not let you suffer any more
than you are able to bear. He is faithful and will find a way for
you to escape so that you will be able to bear it." I sat up with
a look of astonishment and realized that not once had I gone
to the Lord and sought Him in this matter. What a failure! I
knelt before the Lord to ask His forgiveness.

I called my brothers, who were running my business ventures for me, and told them that I would be back to work in
about ten days. At my wife's suggestion, I made a call to her
sister and brother-in-law, Lorna and Doug Petersburg, in Iowa
and asked if I could come and visit for a week or so. They
welcomed me with open arms. They knew that we were having

marital problems and that I was under a lot of business stress, and they had been faithful Barnabas', calling or dropping me notes with encouraging words and Bible verses.

I knew what I needed was a spiritual renewal, and what better place to seek one than a four-hundred-acre farm where there is nothing in sight but fields of corn and soy beans. Most refreshing of all was this young Christian couple who opened their home to me and offered their lovingkindness. They listened quietly as my story unfolded. They'd known something was not right in our marriage, but they never pushed for details. Now I was pouring out my heart.

My wife had not gone to church for about three years. I would get ready every Sunday and go with the kids, but she wouldn't join us. She told me later that she had met someone with whom she spent a lot of time and she felt guilty, so she didn't go. I grieved over the loss of Jesus' message that the house of God is for the weak and sick, not the healthy. I cried to Lorna and Doug and faced the truth. "I don't want to believe what I've heard; I don't want to accuse. I've asked her to go back to church, but she won't."

My dear sister and brother listened attentively. They didn't preach or offer Bible verses; they were just there to love me and spend a lot of time with me.

Each morning I would rise early and go out and see the sun come up so I could recall, "Through the Lord's mercies we are not consumed, because His compassions fail not. They are new every morning; great is Your faithfulness" (Lam. 3:22-23).

Lorna and Doug ran his parents' farm, and I put in a lot of work there, keeping my hands from idleness and letting the Lord deal with my heart. On the third morning, just after the sun came up, my brother-in-law came out and handed me a book entitled, *Prison to Praise*, by Merlin Carruthers. He said, "Sal, why don't you sit and relax today? We've been working pretty hard. Read this and tell me what you think." It was how they witnessed to me of the faithfulness of the Lord. They, knowing that the whole Word was written for every one of my needs, didn't offer any "solve all" verses.

I sat against a telephone pole for over four hours without

moving. As I read, the tears streamed down my cheeks. The theme of the book hammered my head repeatedly:

Rejoice always.
Pray without ceasing.
In everything give thanks; for this is the will of God in Christ Jesus concerning you (I Thess. 5:16-18).

The moment I finished reading, I did just what the book said, and to this day, I have not stopped giving thanks in all things.

Saturday was a big day; we drove by all the neighboring corn fields to see who had the tallest corn stalk. I think that must be a favorite pastime of Iowa farmers. Sunday morning we drove to church, and I was delighted to see a picture-perfect, white building, small and immaculate, with a well-groomed lawn and pretty flowers all around. It was idyllic.

Filling in for the regular pastor was the retired previous pastor. He was a little old man with a soft voice and a gentle spirit. His sermon was fitting and very well-accepted. He and his wife concluded the service by singing a song they had heard on the radio and sent away for the music. It has become one of my favorites.

Come Holy Spirit I need thee
Come sweet spirit I pray
Come in thy strength and thy power
Come in thine own gentle way . . .

Again the tears flowed because I knew what I needed was to be filled with the Holy Spirit. . . . And it did come . . . in its own gentle way.

Later that evening, I witnessed my first midwest thunder-and-lightning storm. The sky was literally lit up, and the noise was frightening. I couldn't sleep, but not because of the storm. I felt there was still some unfinished business. I knelt beside the bed as I went to the throne of grace. I began to thank God for his lovingkindness and tender mercies, and to praise him for his greatness and his majesty. I did this because I knew we were to "enter his gates with thanksgiving and his courts with praise." I just wanted to do everything right this time. God gently reminded me that he must be Lord of all, or not Lord at all.

After that, I felt at total peace and jumped into bed and fell asleep. I think that's what the Scripture means when it refers to the "peace of God that passes all understanding."

Two days later I boarded a plane for Seattle. Little did I know that what God had shown me up to now was only the tip of the iceberg. There would be much more spiritual battle to do, more trips to the hospital, more heartaches, but many more blessings that would not have come about if I had not gone through these trials. God, in all of His wisdom, measures out His love and truth as we are able to receive it to our lives. Never more, never less. It does no good to ask for more, especially if we have not glorified God with what we've already received. It does great harm to ask for less because such a request indicates that God does not know or love or care about us in our condition. God is personally involved in my life, and I am pleased to see His hands mold and shape me—applying pressure, poking, pushing, and soothing me as I need it.

I will never forget what Doug and Lorna Petersburg did for me in Iowa . . . and I will always love them. And in all of God's majesty, He had more than just me in mind as He comforted me in my grief. I have been reminded that no one in his own righteousness is safe from Satan's attacks. I have learned to take my softened heart to my clients as well as to the criminals I am tracking down. If I had not learned to give thanks in everything, I would not have been able to counsel Marilyn Straight's parents in the same way. To God be the glory every time I ask a parent to rejoice evermore or a suspect to pray without ceasing when they fear retaliation from the cult.

We can never know the extent of God's means for any event, but if we make ourselves available to Him to be used in mighty ways, we may receive the blessing of seeing a little of the majesty of His sovereign plan.

After getting this far in my story, no doubt you'll be wondering if I have any kind of a private life other than homicides, ritual killings, deprogrammings, casting out de-

mons, and outrunning attackers, among other things. Well, I
do, and I have had to learn to take time off once in awhile to
maintain my sanity and focus. Not only when I suffer a trial,
but when things are operating routinely also.

The late seventies through early eighties were a real time
of trial for me. Without the Lord in my life, I would not have
survived. I believe he conditioned me early, in Iowa, for the
losses I was endure. God has taught me not to hold on to
anything too tightly, because it hurts that much more when I
have to let go. We are to be loyal to no other commander, no
other foundation, no other god.

I loved my parents dearly. Whenever I was in their neighborhood, I would drop in to have coffee with them. One
morning I stopped by and found both Mom and Dad in tears
and filled with joy. Mom's happy story filtered through her
tears. She explained that she found Dad pacing back and
forth, from the living room to the kitchen. He finally looked
at Mom and said, "Honey, I want you to know that if anything
happens to me, I have made my peace with God. I have
accepted Christ as my savior." Her voice was choked as she
added that, and the tears of joy and the hugs and kisses began
again.

Anytime a soul is saved, it is a time of celebration, but this
woman had a right to celebrate because she had been praying
for Dad and witnessing to him for the full forty-five years of
their marriage. He had been a real hellion all that time.

The very next day, while mowing the lawn, Dad suffered
a stroke that left him speechless and confined him to a wheel-
chair for the remaining year of his life. I believe with all my
heart that for her faithfulness, God allowed Mom to hear
Dad's confession of faith with her own ears.

Two weeks after Dad's death, Mom went totally blind. She
had been a diabetic for several years, and her eyesight had
been failing for sometime. Her health deteriorated rapidly.
Her body was dying, and within a year, she witnessed the
ultimate healing of Christ. Most of her last year was spent in
the hospital. During this time I was going through a divorce,
so I moved closer to the hospital. I was able to spend every
evening with her while she was in there, reading scripture to

her and visiting. She had several different roommates in the hospital over her long stay, and true to form, she would witness to all of them.

On her last day, I arrived at the hospital about 6:30 P.M. and noticed the curtain closed around her bed as I entered the room. I approached quietly and heard the prayer of a dying woman. "Father, I pray that you take me tonight, and I thank you for the full life that you have given me here on earth." There was a silence, so I waited for about two minutes and drew the curtain aside. The broken voice asked, "Is that you, son?"

"Yes, it is," I answered.

"Son, would you read to me about the virtuous woman in Proverbs 31?"

I stayed with Mom until 8:30 P.M.. It was hard to leave, knowing it was my last day with her. I kissed her good-bye and noticed a smile on her face. About two hours later, the hospital called and asked me to come and view the body. (I wrote these words on the seventh anniversary of her death, never really having been able to talk about this in any detail until that time. Any Bible student knows that the number seven holds significance, meaning perfection and completion. I thought then that the Lord had finally perfected this thing in my life. My grieving process was complete.)

Out of us seven children, there was only one brother who was a believer besides myself. My youngest sister, who would eventually come to Christ, was not yet committed to Him at the time of my mother's illness and death. Mom always called on me to visit her. My siblings would spend time with her, too; I'm certainly not trying to make any brownie points, but the truth was that she wanted me there.

Mom and I had a lot in common. We would study the Bible together all the time; I had nothing else to do, and I treasure the opportunity God gave me to do this even in the midst of my sorrow. We shared our joy and our grief and knew we'd be together again in heaven.

I have a place I can go to get away from the pressures; a place I can think, evaluate, but mostly commune with God. My cabin is in central Washington, just twelve miles northeast of

Ellensburg. The cabin is a special place for me because Mom and Dad had purchased the acreage. For two years, they tried to get the entire family up there to see it and have a picnic. One year, Father's Day rolled around, and Dad announced that he wanted no gifts, only for all of us to get together at "Dena's Den." That would be the best gift of all. We all showed up and fell in love with the property and the view. I asked Mom and Dad if they would mind if I built a cabin on the property for use by the entire family. They were delighted.

Three weeks later construction on the cabin was underway, and it was completed in time for the November hunting season. Ever since I was eight years old, Dad had always taken me elk hunting with him. Now we had a place of our own where we could return from the hunt to reasonable comfort, though no electricity or running water.

Now I felt a need to get away as the losses seemed to be stacking up like cord wood. I sought the face of Almighty God at the foot of the beautiful pines and evergreens. "Father, could this be Your will for me?" I asked. The absolutes began to run through my mind as I let the Holy Spirit minister to me. God is still Lord. . . . He is still on his throne. . . . Live or die, I still belong to Him. . . . The Lord gives, and the Lord takes away; blessed be the name of the Lord. Scripture began jumping out at me like flashing neon lights.

> For I know the thoughts that I think toward you, says
> the Lord, thoughts of peace and not of evil, to give you
> a future and a hope. Then you will call upon Me and
> go and pray to Me, and I will listen to you. And you will
> seek Me and find Me, when you search for Me with all
> your heart. (Jer. 29:11-13)

I knew I had the promises, but still the understanding evaded me. Then the verse jumped out at me, "'For My thoughts are not your thoughts, nor are your ways My ways,' says the Lord" (Isa. 55:8). I realized that in time I may understand, but then I may not. Mine was not to understand, but to trust. I began to "put on the garment of praise for the spirit of heaviness." I remembered my trip to Iowa and the verses that would stick with me:

Rejoice always.

Pray without ceasing.

In everything give thanks, for this is the will of God in Christ Jesus concerning you.

There I had my answer; nothing happens in the life of a believer without the Lord allowing it.

I still manage to get to my cabin about two or three times a year. Usually my son and I go up to bow hunt and carry on the father-son tradition. What a precious time. My love for my parents, the time I spent with my mom before her passing into the arms of Jesus, all crystallized in my approach to my work and my children.

My daughter was a teen-ager when her parents divorced, and she spent a great deal of these years of maturing into an adult with me. She is a believer today at twenty-six years old. My son is now nineteen; we adopted him when he was almost five years old. He lives with his mother near Tacoma, and we visit together often, watching movies, bow hunting, or reading scriptures together. He has always loved to talk, especially to hear my stories about funny, embarrassing times in my life.

We sit by the fire and discuss the Bible and Christian living, and my son listens as I try to impress upon him the importance of a man knowing and loving the Lord and His word. He knows he will be thankful in years to come for these talks today. He tells me now, "Dad, those are the best times of my life. I'll never forget that. Whenever I'm in trouble, whenever I need to think about something nice in my life, I think about those times." It is such a reward to hear this from my son, my greatest gift to God.

My children provide me with reminders everyday that life is precious. I remember their delight and love for the Lord as I listen to the sorrowful stories of parents who have lost their sons or daughters to Satan, either directly through the occult, or indirectly through rebellion.

The first thing I did after I myself became a believer and promised to do what He wanted me to do—not what I wanted to do as my emotions ran amok—was commit to share the love of Christ with even the worst criminal, even if it was my own flesh and blood whose life had been taken. There is not one convicted or accused killer whom I have not told that I loved them and given them a hug if they let me. I never left them without informing them not only that I loved them, but the Lord of all loved them.

> This poor man cried out, and the Lord heard him, and saved him out of all his troubles. The angel of the Lord encamps all around those who fear Him, and delivers them. Oh, taste and see that the Lord is good: blessed is the man who trusts in Him. (Ps. 34:6-8)

God has sent angels (real or mortals with heavenly compassion) to me throughout my career. As I mentioned earlier, Christians came out of the woodwork whenever I would publicly voice my source of strength. When I spoke in secular surroundings, Christians added to the effort to demonstrate God's glory. In Atlanta, pastors and congregations prayed for me unceasingly. Every major city hosts a Christian Peace Officer Association (or the like), and they assist in the investigation sometimes by taking on particular duties, but always by providing spiritual encouragement. This especially helped in Atlanta, but so did the Christ-like support given by an angel with a clear, melodious voice.

During the trial, all or part of the defense team would lunch across the street from the courthouse at a half-sit-down, half-cafeteria style restaurant. In the middle of the restaurant was a piano where a fortyish woman would play some mellow tunes and an occasional gospel song. I could tell she loved the Lord by the peace, joy, and love she transmitted through her music and her engaging smile.

One day she played an all-time favorite of mine, "It Is Well With My Soul." It had been my mother's favorite and was sung at her funeral. As she played, I stopped and turned toward her. She saw that the music had touched me deeply. She smiled in a comforting way and ministered to me with her song. When she finished, I went to her and thanked her.

"Do you have a request, Mr. Dena?" She explained that she had seen me on the news and knew my name. My request was "How Great Thou Art." She answered that she would play it if I would help her, and she motioned me to share the piano bench with her.

We started out a bit softly but increased our volume as a few people yelled, "Louder." The pressure of the trial, my marriage, and the endless looking over of my shoulder for those who would do me harm was taking a toll on me. God knew what I needed that day, a gentle reminder that He was watching over me and that I was not forgotten. The phrase "And God remembered . . . " appears a number of times in the Bible, each time as one of His own suffered despair and sorrow. Noah, Abraham, Rachel, the sons of Israel, Hannah— all experienced the sure and soothing comfort of God expressed in Hebrews 6:10: "For God is not unjust to forget your work and labor of love which you have shown toward His name, in that you have ministered to the saints, and do minister."

He used the woman at the piano and all those who applauded our impromptu concert to accomplish His will. That's the way my God works, never late, always on time with His remembrance.

In the Trenches

[Senior devil Screwtape to junior devil Wormwood:] "Whatever men expect, they soon come to think they have a right to; the sense of disappointment can, with very little skill on our part, be turned into a sense of injury."—C.S. Lewis, *Screwtape Letters*

Learning the tools of the trade as an investigator into occult-related crime has involved more than just following footprints or tracking clues. And it has required more than the heart-changes I've talked about. I have needed to learn how to collect the resources that will make the job go more smoothly, such as selecting the right personnel to work with me, executing the operations demanded by my clients, and effecting good communication skills. All of my work would be so much easier, however, if I didn't have to deal with the posturing of those within the church who are trying to score theological points on one side of an issue or the other: specifically whether all the talk about satanism is just whipping up unnecessary hysteria among God's people.

I'm bothered by Christians making wild claims of satanic attack or demon possession, or anyone who goes overboard in the name of religion, without any substantiation for their stories. I have had people come to me stating that they have identified as many as forty-seven demons in a person, including the demons of dandruff and bad breath, etc., etc., which they, of course, have been good enough to cast out.

I must tell you that I have a problem with this. I think it does more harm than good when someone claims that God has visited them personally to give them a message or they are doing battle with the demon of halitosis. We need to recognize that this is simply an effort to remove blame from themselves for all things, much less poor bodily cleanliness habits, and put it on Satan. "Satan made me eat this and now I've gained ten pounds" can escalate into "Satan made me kill that person."

I believe the greatest danger is in unknowingly leading others into this trap through careless words and actions. By simply saying things the way we intend them to be interpreted can help us escape this problem. The Bible spends a great deal of space discussing the importance of ruling the tongue. There's a reason for this. Overstatement, misstatement, and understatement about God and His word probably aids Satan more than any other activity—even outright ritualistic worship.

Beloved, let me say this to you in a loving way, STOP IT! Read your Bible. Don't listen to what man says, go to the scriptures. Don't just take my word on the subject. See what the scriptures say and let the Holy Spirit guide you.

Over-sensationalizing the existence of Satan and his agenda hurts my business. So does under-reporting it. Oh, I know it will be easy for critics to say that the reason I say this is because if it weren't for alleged satanism and occultism, I wouldn't have a job. Not so. I don't need to do what I do for an income. I have plenty of other sources for a paycheck. I do this because I believe God has made it clear in His word that this activity does exist and He has given me the talents to expose it and halt it before it does any damage to God's work.

My critics may believe that I should relish all the emphasis the media and the church place on satanism because of the business it brings. On the contrary, I operate only within the truth, as any good investigator does. I'm trained to do this, and I'd be out of business if I didn't. Unfortunately, it's a training too few within the church have been willing to put themselves through. One of the biggest problems is that "lazy" Christians will listen to someone who claims to have a little bit of background on a subject and not hold the information—or the speaker—to any accountability checks. No one verifies the facts. It's especially true in this field. People do not take the time to find scripture that addresses the subject.

The upshot of this comes when too many people rely on what one person is saying on a subject, providing fertile ground for the beginning of a cult. I have seen folks who are so eager to believe in *something* that a real smooth talker could get them to worship a head of cabbage named "Ralph" in just a matter of minutes.

A funny incident occurred in the mid-seventies. I was working for a family that had a daughter who had gotten involved with the Unification Church in Seattle—the Moonies. Her ex-boyfriend was just as anxious to get her back and made himself available to be used by me in anyway I needed him.

My job was to get into the Moonies' big home in Windemere, the most affluent part of town, kidnap her, and reunite her with her family. Then we'd get her into counseling. This young man kept his gray cells exercised and used his head in this case. He ran some surveillance on the house on his own and laid out the situation for me. He found that there were sixteen to twenty Moonies there at any one time, and his girlfriend was definitely in the house.

Nearby were swamps where miles of skunk cabbage grew. He put a head of skunk cabbage by the window of her room. Occasionally they let her talk to him on the phone, and she would express that her greatest desire was to see him come to "the Lord." Once in one of these conversations, he told her that he had a dream in which God had spoken to him. She was so excited to hear this. He continued and told her that in the dream God told him that the Antichrist was coming; they would know it was the Antichrist because the smell of skunk would permeate the area. Once she detected that smell, he warned her, she should know that she was surrounded by the Antichrist. Lo and behold, he was the one I credit for getting her out of that cult.

Those same "fierce wolves" of the pack are here today, as the scripture says (Matt. 7:6), and they are trying to see how many people they can deceive. As a child, my father taught me to "believe nothing of what you hear and only half of what you see." I think that was good counsel. Even today as a Christian investigator, I look at the facts, check the scriptures, test the spirits, meditate on the word, but I still keep my powder dry.

> The harvest truly is plenteous, but the laborers are few. Therefore pray the Lord of the harvest to send out laborers into his harvest . . . For many are called, but few are chosen. (Matt. 9:37,38; 20:16)

Shortly after the "Ted" case broke, I was so busy that I needed help in my agency. Several police officers whom I had met in the course of my investigations had already contacted me, wanting part-time work. Some were close to retirement and others were already retired who wanted full-time work. I was doing 95 percent criminal investigations and 5 percent domestic work for attorney friends of mine and other personal associates who had needs. I needed someone immediately to do my leg work and free me for other aspects of the work.

While in college, I became good friends with a student in my karate class. He was very interested in the martial arts. Before long, he and his new bride both joined the class, and both went on to get their black belts. Only a small percentage of those who study karate are awarded a black belt; it takes time and dedication. I knew then that Ric and Jan Landon were special and would be lifelong friends.

Ric wanted to work with me, and his background with a small local police force was appealing, but one main reservation held me back. The type of work I had been doing for the past year or so was the investigation into the occult, satanism, and witchcraft. Ric was not a believer. I felt I needed to hire a Christian so that he would be able to understand the spiritual world and be able to do battle with Satan in his own back yard.

I stopped to remember my promise to God and to recall the primary function of a believer: to win souls for Christ. I took Ric on board and showed him what I did and what I believed to be the answer. He went with me on my speaking engagements and continued to learn and to study.

Eventually Jan accepted Christ, but Ric was a little harder to convince. A short time later, their first son was born, and I was asked to be the godfather. "Before I say yes and tell you how flattered I am, I have a question. Why me?"

"Because," Ric said, "If something ever happened to us, we know how you would raise our son. We know you would take him to church and teach him about God." Then I looked at Ric and asked, "If God is good enough for your son, why isn't he good enough for you?" The look on his face said it all. He knew, and I knew that he was facing a decision; God's compelling ways had brought him to this point.

A few days later, we had a case in Anchorage which called for three of us to journey up there and do some investigation. The other part-time detective was a full-time pastor. It was 26 below in Anchorage, and we were in a hurry to finish our work and get home. One evening while we were having dinner at a nice restaurant on the water, enjoying a steak and Alaskan King crab legs, I noticed that Ric was extremely quiet while Don and I discussed the case and other cases back home. A few minutes later, I noticed a few tears in Ric's eyes, and then a few tears hit the table. I knew what was happening, and I reached over and put my hand on his shoulder. I didn't say a word; nothing had to be said.

We finished our job in Anchorage, leaving the bitter cold to come home to the drizzling rain. A few days later, I received a call from Jan, thanking me for the gift. "What gift?" I asked.

"The new husband you brought home from Anchorage," she said.

Don Vanderbecken, the other detective on that case accompanied me to a number of the speaking engagements I would take on with Shirley Landa of the Citizens Freedom Foundation in Washington. Don left his work as a pastor of custodial care at a large church in Seattle to enter counseling work, and then considered pursuing an investigator's license so that he could come work with me. He was so stunned by what he witnessed as my assistant that he eventually quit. This is no indictment of him or his intentions. Don was a perfect example of someone with a biblical, seminary background who was frightened away from learning any more about satanism than he already knew.

One day he and I were to meet. He had a box of books and materials about the occult in the trunk of his car. On the way to our meeting, he got into an accident. Don believes to this day that Satan caused the accident in order to get him out of the work. When he told me this, I looked at him a little strangely and said, "Well, Don, that could be, but I don't know that I totally agree with that." There was no dissuading him. He left my agency and began work in a field with no ties to the church; his faith is still strong; he still studies the Word. He just got scared by some admittedly scary stuff.

Without a doubt, when interviewing people to work with me, I have encountered a wide range of responses when I begin to describe the work. Many non-believers tend to raise their brows, only interested when it pertains to grizzly homicides. Others take it very seriously. These I spot pretty quickly and take the opportunity to witness that we need the Lord, God is in control, and all is not lost.

In the past twenty years, I have had over twenty detectives, and if they were not Christians when I hired them, they were within a very short time. I believe if you are going to work on spiritual matters, you must be spiritually minded in order to understand the situation. My rule of thumb on this subject is if one spends one hour looking into the occult, satanism, or witchcraft, one should spend two hours in the word. I warn you, this field is not for everyone.

As many of my detectives came to the understanding of the deadly realm of the occult, I wish that many law enforcement authorities did as well in those early years. It would have made my job a lot easier. Now manuals abound among police departments and task forces offering advice and direction in dealing with satanism, the occult, and witchcraft. In those days, however, even the slightest hint that anything spiritual was involved in a situation brought on comments about "wackos"—referring to the one doing the hinting—and imminent closure of the case because of the religious element.

A lot of times the way I have to go about investigating a case requires me to engage in activities that the police themselves would never do. Of course, most of the time the reason they can't is because it would indicate the case had been prejudged by the courts. Very simply, they wouldn't be able to get search warrants on the little bit of evidence I work with.

Because I don't have on me the restriction of representing the authorities (just the truth), I have more leeway in my investigations. I very often gain access to materials, evidence, and documents through methods which I have no intention in divulging here or anywhere.

> Bring no more futile sacrifices; incense is an abomination to Me. Your New Moons, the Sabbaths, and the calling of assemblies—I cannot endure iniquity and the sacred meeting. Your New Moons and your appointed feasts My soul hates; they are a trouble to Me, I am weary of bearing them. When you spread out your hands, I will hide My eyes from you; even though you make many prayers, I will not hear. Your hands are full of blood. Wash yourselves, make yourselves clean; put away the evil of your doings from before My eyes. Cease to do evil. (Isa. 1:13-16)

By now, the calls were coming in by the dozens for cult deprogrammings. A number of the assignments included me physically removing loved ones from cult groups. I was extremely cautious since there had been others who in doing what I did had been arrested for kidnapping and false imprisonment. I don't do much in this area now, but from 1975 to 1985 it was the most oft requested service in the detective agency. Eventually I had to decide if my work should be centered more in the area of cult investigations or the occult, and since so many had begun to hang out their shingle in cult deprogrammings, I felt sure my talent was needed in investigating the occult.

A close friend and associate in the work was Shirley Landa, one of those rare people with an untiring stamina; she was previously associated with the Spiritual Counterfeits Project in Berkeley, California. Once she starts a project, she sees it through to its completion. Shirley and I started deprogramming at the same time since it was her son's deprogramming that brought us together. Her son was taken by a small religious cult in about 1974. Before too long, Shirley was mostly doing deprogrammings in the office and a lot of research on cult groups. I did most of the field work and deprogrammings on the ones we could not get into the office.

By the summer of 1975, we had identified a number of cult groups just west of the mountains in the state of Washington alone. This did not include satanists, occult groups, or witch covens. Shirley's organization, Citizens Freedom Foundation, of which she was the head, received a number of phone calls from people asking about groups operating in their communities, and our agency would check them out. It amazed me that so many of these callers had already contacted the police and were told the authorities could not investigate because it involved religious matters. "We do know of an investigator," the police would say, and we'd hear from them next. After just one year we had researched 150 groups.

Shirley and her husband George have devoted a lot of time and money of their own for the research of cult groups and the deprogramming of cult captives. They are to be commended for their unselfish attitude. Without their input and hard work, I would have had fewer success stories than I did. Of course, there is no way to really know whether one has been successful in a deprogramming. There are so many variables that can effect the outcome: the approach of the deprogrammer, how long the individual was in the group, how deeply he or she was involved. If we didn't stay on top of the situation and meet with the individual every few days, they would go back to the cult. We called this the "floating" stage. It would be so easy to lose someone in this stage; a simple phone call from a friend in the group would cause them to float back. I am certain that continual counseling is the best deterrent to this gravitational pull the cult group has on the individual.

I have had a lot of people question my credentials in handling this type of work. One would think that a psychologist or psychiatrist would be the best person to perform a deprogramming. I don't think that's true. In my estimation, a

Bible-believing Christian would provide the best counseling because of the deep spiritual nature of the control the cults exercise over the individual.

> Chasten your son while there is hope, and do not set
> your heart on his destruction. (Prov. 19:18)

Narcotics work has always been exhausting and both physically and emotionally draining for me. As a rule, the higher the value of the drugs you are dealing with, the greater the danger you will be faced with. For the most part, it can be thankless; there have been very few rewarding experiences. However, there are some that are worth writing about.

Because I had had a problem with alcohol when I returned from military duty overseas, I can identify with an addiction. I knew that there had been something lacking in my life to propel me toward drink in order to satisfy this void and escape reality. For these kids, I understood that there was a reason behind their habits. Even though all my job required was for me to get them to the drug rehabilitation center, I wanted to take it a step further and see what I could do to help these kids a little. I desired to minister to them as someone who had been there and got out because I wanted to. God could make them want to, too. More so, I witnessed to them.

The parents of a young man called me because their seventeen-year-old son had been using marijuana and cocaine. He was also an alcoholic. They had taken him to an outpatient facility at least twice and found it to be unsatisfactory. Now, they were faced with intervention. At the time, to their knowledge, there were only three lock-up facilities in the U.S. Arrangements had been made at a facility in Minneapolis for admissions on a particular day. These facilities were extremely difficult to get someone into, with a standard six- to twelve-month waiting period.

The problem was getting the boy to Minneapolis. He was not willing to go on his own.

I met with the parents to see what they were like. This would help me size up the job. I found two loving Christians who adored their two sons. They were heartbroken and in tears.

My first question to them was, "Are you willing to thank God for the situation we are in right now?" They looked at me in a strange way, not believing what they had just heard. "The scriptures say that we are to give thanks in all things, and I say 'we' because I am committed to Christ and to you in this situation."

"I don't think I understand," the father said. I explained that if God, in his infinite wisdom, had allowed this to happen, then it was for a purpose. Our job was to trust and obey. We were all in agreement, so now it was time to let the Lord guide us.

My new associate Ed Bueser and I showed up at their home one evening around eight. We were warned that the boy would put up a fight. Earlier that day, I went before the Lord and told him how I was afraid that I might hurt the boy if he gave us too much trouble. That was the last thing I wanted to do. "Father," I prayed, "If this is your will, then I'm ready to go where you send me, do what you want me to do, and say what you want me to say, but I must admit that I'm a little unsure of myself, so my eyes are on you."

Now I know why God sent Ed to me. Ed and I have been friends for several years. He was a new student in our karate class who went on to earn his black belt. On top of that, he had a good sense of humor—something that is very important in this business. It was his idea to play the "good guy, bad guy" routine.

As we approached the boy's downstairs bedroom, we noticed that the door was vibrating from the loud music inside. We walked in and found the walls plastered with pornography, and empty booze bottles were lined up all around the perimeter of the room. The boy was lying on his bed reading a porno book. I unplugged the stereo, and with a smile on my face, I introduced the two of us.

"Son, this is Ed Bueser and my name is Sal Dena. We are here to escort you to an all-expenses-paid vacation to a drug rehab center in Minneapolis." He looked surprised and angry all at once. "Now before you say anything," I said, "You can go one of two ways, either in the trunk or the front seat. It's up to you."

Ed stepped between us and whispered to him, loud enough for me to hear, "Don't make him mad, he's an animal." I cracked my knuckles and threw karate chops into the air. I knew I must have looked like a cartoon figure.

"I think I would like to go in the front seat," he said. "I'm not dumb enough to fight you two." Once we got outside, I warned him, "Now if you try and make a break for it, I will personally rip your arms out at the sockets and beat you with the bloody stumps." Wherever we went after that, he was very careful to keep Ed between us. The hardest thing for me to do was to maintain a straight face through this whole ordeal.

We boarded the flight and arrived in Minneapolis with not so much as a peep from our young man. We picked up our rental car and drove to the rehab center. As the boy's father was checking him in, the staff took us on a tour of the facility. We were very impressed.

When it was time to say good-bye to the boy, I asked him if there was anything he needed. "Gum," he answered, so I bought several packages for him. We were finally face to face when I saw a tear in his eye. I could see that he didn't want me to go; he knew that he needed a bully, an authority figure to tell him what to do, and to care about him at the same time. I began to cry as I gave him a big hug and promised to pray for him. For me it was a very touching moment. I hadn't fooled him for a minute; he knew I was a cream puff.

A few months later he was released and came home to Seattle to his parents' home. He called me to make arrangements to meet and collect the hamburger and fries I had promised him. With the exception of a couple of small steps backward, he has done quite well and I am very proud of him. His parents and I see each other occasionally and have become very good friends. They have begun leading drug dependency seminars and have grown spiritually by leaps and bounds.

This case began with me asking the parents if they could give thanks in this situation. They could not understand, but they did it. Now it was time for God to put the finishing touches on the situation, according to the scripture: "For this is the will of God in Christ Jesus concerning you" (I Thess. 5:18).

Beloved, do not think it strange concerning the fiery
trial which is to try you, as though some strange thing
happened to you; but rejoice to the extent that you
partake of Christ's sufferings, that when His glory is
revealed, you may also be glad with exceeding joy. (I
Pet. 4:12,13)

Try it, you'll like it.

Another similar case was just as rewarding. This young
man was also seventeen and with much the same dependen-
cies. The parents warned us that this one would be our "worst
nightmare." They had made the mistake of threatening the
boy with the horror story of enlisting the help of the two
gorillas who walked on the edges of their feet and whose
knuckles dragged on the ground. That is the reputation that
Ed and I had gained from all of the patients in the same
intervention program.

The parents made the threat, and the boy locked himself
in his room for two weeks with a loaded shotgun waiting for
"Bozo" and "Bonzo" to appear. Finally he gave up his vigil and
had almost forgotten about us.

On the last day of school, at about 6 A.M., we entered his
bedroom, woke him up, and introduced ourselves. He began
screaming, punching, kicking, yelling, cussing, spitting—all at
once. This time it took three of us. Nothing I could say or do
would calm him down, so I covered his mouth and explained
who we were and where we were going. I told him he could
fight all he wanted, but he was going, even if I had to knock
him out; he would go. There was no other option.

He began crying very loudly and cursing his parents as we
removed him from the home. I later learned that his greatest
fear was not knowing what we would do to him. He cried all
the way to Minneapolis and continued to do so as he disappeared with the orderlies at the rehab center.

Several months went by before I heard from the boy's
parents. He was doing fine and was on his way home. I had
continued to pray for him every time I thought of him. Then
finally payday came when I received a note from him. It read,
"Thank you for doing for me what I could not do for myself;
God bless." A few months later I saw him on educational T.V.,

working with a drug rehabilitation center, urging young people to stay away from drugs.

No amount of money could have been better payment than this. God Bless you Mike and David!

The Wiles of the Devil

> We know from his [Milton's] prose works that he believed everything detestable to be, in the long run, also ridiculous; and mere Christianity commits every Christian to believing that "the Devil is (in the long run) an ass."—C.S. Lewis, preface to *Paradise Lost*

Even though worship of Satan in our nation is constitutionally protected, the criminal acts which accompany the worship rituals of a majority of groups who claim devotion to Satan are not. I would like to say that I trust man enough to, once educated on the issues, be able to choose the correct path for living. But I don't trust man that much. I can't even trust man a little—myself included. The Bible says, "The heart is deceitful above all things, and desperately wicked; who can know it?" (Jer. 17:9). Were it not for God putting me on the path of righteousness, I would be no where near it.

It has been this false idea that man can be left to determine what is good for him that has led to the infiltration of satanism, occultism and witchcraft into our twentieth-century society. The popular notion is that if we present everything evenly to our children in schools, they will be able to make healthy decisions. The proponents of such measures refuse to see the evidence, but it has already been documented over and over again that such exercises are ruining a whole generation of young people who need and want more direction than that. It's been the practice with drug education, sex education, and now New Age education. The resounding cry is for pluralism—let every voice be heard; the good will stand, and the bad will wither away. History has shown us clearly that this is not so; the Bible is even more adamant that man's heart cannot even know how wicked it is. Plurality always brings chaos. I have seen it first hand.

> I will never leave you nor forsake you. . . . The Lord is
> my helper; I will not fear. What can man do to me?
> (Heb. 13:5,6)

After returning from the midwest, I was called by a group of people who said they had a satanic group in their area. Some of their children had seen the group kill a dog in a ritual ceremony in a building south of Seattle. After four weeks of surveillance, I was able to get the names, license numbers, and the addresses of everyone in the group. Awhile later, I witnessed the decapitation of another dog, as well as their cutting the dog open and removing some organs.

There had been several reports made to the Kent police department. The group in question had done nothing wrong (Animal rights activists had not bucked heads with the paganists yet.); no crime had been committed, so the police couldn't do anything. The people in the neighborhood were frightened, and they felt threatened and intimidated, but nothing could be done.

When the weather was nice, the same group would hold rituals along the Green River in a grassy area at night. They used gas to make an outline of a baphomet (an upside down pentagram, or five-pointed star) and lit it. They would then jump into the circle and do a ritual dance. This was followed by an orgy and extensive drug use. After one of the orgies, I followed two couples to a motel where they were staying.

I must have been following them too closely because they recognized my car from back by the river. As soon as we were in the parking lot, the two guys pulled guns and headed toward me. I was already out of my car when I saw the guns so I looked for cover. I ran for the nearby cornfield that filled an entire area between the parking lot and the Green River (about one thousand yards). God provides; the cornrows ran parallel to the direction I was heading.

The first round went zinging over my left shoulder. I began to zig zag so that I would be a harder target to hit, knocking down corn stalks on my left and right as I plowed like a madman to get away from my pursuers. The second round blasted even louder than the first (larger caliber). Then I heard one yell to the other, "Keep him between us; don't let him get to your outside." A third round, then a fourth round went zinging by.

Oh Lord, make haste to help me, I thought, and suddenly the bank of the river was in front of me. There was no time to think, just jump. The thought ran through my mind, *Trust in the Lord with all thine heart, lean not unto thine own understanding. In all thy ways acknowledge Him and He shall direct thy path.* It was pitch black out beyond the embankment, and there was about a fifteen-foot drop to the water. I had no idea how deep the river was this time of year and absolutely no clue as to what kind of debris I could expect to find when I hit.

I landed with a loud splash. The river was just about five feet deep. I quickly made my way to the opposite side and hid in the overgrown grass that spread down to the edge of the water. In silence I waited as my pursuers made their way to the water bank. In a few minutes, they gave up the chase and headed back through the corn.

I stood and remained still for several minutes. In amazement I inspected the place where I had landed. There were several loose stumps that were stuck together at the bend of the river. My landing place in the middle of this was about as big around as my dining room table. My body finding that hole was like finding a needle in a haystack.

I decided to leave my car in the parking lot and walk home. They had my license number and made good on it. I had expected a reprisal from my evening's activities—they didn't let me down. A number of threatening phone calls came in for a few weeks, but there were no physical attacks.

The case was never handled by the police. You see, there was never any activity beyond animal sacrifices and mutilations being performed by this group, and both King County police and Kent police had policies against interfering in anything that appeared religious in nature. The bizarre was being tolerated.

With the emergence of so many cult groups, it was difficult to know at any one time what kind of group we were dealing with and what they believed in. I realized then that I didn't need to know what they believed in, but what the Bible taught, and if I knew what the Word said, I would be able to spot the phony teachings at a glance. My job, as I saw it, was to identify these groups, find out who their leader was, and to determine what area of town they were operating in. That way, when people called me about a particular group, I could give them a little background about it.

Animal mutilations were occurring quite frequently in our area, but mostly in the suburbs. When a mutilation would occur in the city, I would usually get a call from the humane society and the police department. One such dog mutilation occurred on the northwest side of town. A decapitated and skinned dog hung by wires on the front porch of a house. It was also missing its sexual organs.

The police concluded that someone was tired of hearing the dog bark and put an end to its life. I knew this was not so. I had seen this before, and I knew it was a warning. I checked with the police department to see if there had been any complaints in the neighborhood of bizarre practices such as witchcraft or satanism. Sure enough, there had been complaints of that very thing in the recent past. I also checked on the people living in the house where the dog was found and checked their background for the past few years. I found that they had reputedly been involved in the occult. The problem was that there were already people living in the neighborhood who belonged to a witch coven and didn't like outsiders invading their space. Now, try explaining all this to the authorities. Nothing could be proven, and again the police department had its hands tied by policy. These were incidents of a religious nature and a form of worship.

Animal mutilations continued, and I continued to view as many as I possibly could. A few of my police friends would call and inform me of a new incident so I could see it as fresh as possible. I began noticing a few differences in certain mutilations. They would differ from one geographical area to another, time of year, or month, and what part of the animal was mutilated. For instance, sometimes I would find horses or cows with missing tongues or eyes, and sometimes the sexual organs were missing. Once in a while, I would find a heart or the feet missing.

After talking with several people who had come out of one of those groups, I found that they were about 95 percent consistent as to their explanations of what happens. I've discovered that the rituals always correspond to a certain time of year—days of ritual and celebration, and they regularly follow a proscribed method of worship. Sometimes the ritual demands that they plant the feet, drink the blood, incinerate the body parts, or devour the sexual organs—all in attempts to gain more power and energy in their worship. The larger the animal, the more power they gain.

It is possible now for me to see a mutilation and be able to determine whether a satanic group or witchcraft is responsible, which particular group is involved, and what type of worship they were performing.

I knew the day would come when I would be called in to view the remains of human mutilations, and sure enough it happened. Police departments are very cautious about how much they should reveal in cases like this, and rightly so. Some departments are too proud to enlist help from an outside source for something like this. Amazingly, while they shun the offers of assistance from conservative, conscientious investigators like myself, they will call on psychics and clairvoyants and think nothing of asking for help from charlatans.

I have had calls to view bodies that have been axed, decapitated, and mutilated beyond recognition, or stabbed repeatedly with a knife or screwdriver, the weapon still intact. I have seen bodies that were obviously eaten by animals, and there is no possible way of determining the cause of death. These of course were not ritual killings, but were very often murders committed to silence an individual or warn others. In the end it is extremely difficult to find a body of a person who was a victim of a satanic ritual because they are usually burned or otherwise destroyed.

Convenient, isn't it? It seems to play into the hands of those who claim that all this talk about satanism is creating a hysteria about something that can't be proved. Missing bodies are a problem. But these groups rely upon secrecy for security of existence. If a body is found, it is for the purpose of scaring the community and giving credence to the group. Probably the best thing that could happen to indicate the extent of the problem of satanism, the occult, or witchcraft is for the media to make national news out of every case. The public would know just how often it occurs, and those most likely to succumb to satanism hysteria would have information to go on and not just rumors.

Victims of a witchcraft ritual who have been decapitated or dismembered are usually left to be found so as to put fear in those who find the remains. They may also serve as a sacrifice to a particular god, such as earth, stars, moon, water, wind, etc. This, however, does not always hold true, because not all groups worship alike. Each new coven leader may use the traditional format then add to or take away from the original worship as they see fit.

> Are not two sparrows sold for a copper coin? And not one of them falls to the ground apart from your Father's will. (Matt. 10:29)

One element of satanism, the occult, and witchcraft that regularly shows up in my investigations of occult-related crimes were the family ties—either among family members in the same occult group, family or spouses keeping a member's activities secret, or violence perpetrated against family members for the purpose of fulfilling a ritualistic demand.

I was still reeling from the Wayne Williams case—an example of family complicity—when a call came from a man I had met a few years before, during my days of karate competition.

His daughter had been brutally murdered in his home,

and the police had no leads. Because of the proximity of his home to the airport strip, he felt that she could have been a victim of the Green River killer. The Green River killings had started a short time before this one, and all of the victims had been taken from the airport strip just blocks away.

The homicide scene was a bloody mess. The victim was face down on the dining room floor. A sixteen-inch butcher knife was embedded in her back, a second knife next to it. A third knife was found a few feet away near the fireplace. At a first glance, the knives would appear to be the murder weapons, but not so in this case.

There were also blood splatters in a large X-pattern on the ceiling. Under the victim's head was a pool of blood, and under her black, curly hair were several lacerations on the right side of the skull. The medical examiner concluded that a wooden clublike object with beveled edges appeared to be the murder weapon. His description fit the description of "nunchakus," commonly called "chaku sticks" by martial artists. They are two sticks made of hard wood with beveled edges, joined together with a small chain or a thin rope. The victim's entire family and all their friends were involved in the martial arts, so the killer could have been any one of a number of people.

A short time after the divorce of her parents, the girl started going to church and, soon after, accepted Christ as her savior. The rest of the family were not believers. After doing a little digging, I found out she was a little "slow"—not retarded, but what today would be called "learning disabled." She had joined a Bible study and was active in her church. From what her family had told me, she had worked very hard at witnessing to each of them, but none of them took her seriously.

This is the kind of investigation that is gut-wrenching to me. More than that, it really tugs at my heartstrings. To think that this young girl, hurting so badly from the breakup of her family, in her pain seeks and encounters the Lord's call and turns to serve Him. Her ministry begins at home as she witnesses to the rest of her family then continues to grow in Christ by attending Bible classes and seeking the godly life.

Her life is then cut short here on earth at the hands of a cold-blooded killer. I have tears every time I think of this case.

At the onset, I saw something I didn't like. The possibility that the killer was a relative continued to hang over the case. Both the brother and father were involved in Kung Fu. I had known them in the karate circles, but not as well as I thought I did. A slightly built, muscular young man, the brother thought more highly of himself than the rest of us did. He and his father were always showy and egotistical in everything they did, playing up to the ninja persona, dressing like a character in a kids' show. But he was never a force to contend with in martial arts circles.

The police could not really lean on anyone too hard, but I could because I was hired by the family. I must have stepped on some toes, because I soon had some shadows. On the third day of being followed, they jumped me as I was getting home late.

After I parked my car in my numbered stall, I headed down the walkway toward my apartment. I noticed that the overhead spotlight at the end of the building was out. The apartment management was always quick to repair any problems, so this alerted me to potential danger. The large shrubs on either side of the walkway gave perfect cover and concealment. All of a sudden, I was hit from behind, first in the ribs, then the head.

I spun around guarding my head. Immediately I noticed that my attacker had the moves of a martial artist, of one particular martial artist. He moved in quickly for another strike. Just then, I darted forward as fast as I could with a well-placed, front snap kick that buckled him. He knew he couldn't take me by himself. I reached for the .45 tucked in my belt at my back and pulled it out just as a second attacker came at me. After seeing the barrel of my automatic in his face, he stopped in his tracks. What the heck, I gave him a kick and put him on his back too. It's funny what survivalist instincts come out in a person. In a blink of an eye, I reverted back to my marine corps days.

I pulled off their masks and said, "Okay girls, I want some answers now. I am about to beat you two severely about the head and shoulders. If you tell me what I want to hear, I may let you live." I got my answers and sent them on their way. It was all I could do to get in my car and drive myself to the hospital. The tough talk is always part of the job; unfortunately so is the abuse I get.

It wouldn't have done any good to say anything to the police about this incident. "They didn't like you, Sal. You were putting your nose where it didn't belong."

To this day, that case remains unsolved. One of the hardest things to accept in this work is to know who the guilty party is and not have the proof to put them away. My only consolation is in the fact that they will face judgment like the rest of us, but this time, they will not fool the judge and jury.

It was clear there was an element of evil at play here. A young Christian girl, her heart made pure by the atoning blood of her savior, could not be allowed to exist in the midst of wickedness propelled by a hatred of that same Christ.

In a similar vein, I had a murder investigation which developed at the same time as the Vonnie Stuth case surfaced. The victim was not quite thirty when he was found in a ditch with his hands tied behind his back and a 9mm. slug through the back of his head. Six thousand dollars was wadded in his front pocket, a drug deal gone bad. I knew there were no occult or satanic aspects to this case, but I was fascinated with the complexity of the elements. Since my background was in narcotics investigation, I stuck to it.

As we looked into his death, we came across the murder weapon in the suspect's home, and we ran a ballistics check on it. We couldn't go on the positive match to the slug in his brain, because we didn't have enough probable cause to get a search warrant to obtain the weapon legally. I really believed we'd find the suspect who killed him and be able to solve the case, but nothing ever happened. Today, the deceased's wife is married to the suspect.

If Satan can't get the family to be his accomplices in chaos and havoc, he will try another sphere: the church.

I have a dear friend who is a born-again believer with firsthand knowledge on this subject. Several years ago, she was a satanist high priestess. Her job as a Satanist was not to don ceremonial robes and participate in rituals. It was very simple. She was to infiltrate all those churches that were "on fire" for the Lord. The hotter the church, the more critical it was for Satan to get a foothold. She would join the church and go through all the motions: join a Bible study, attend the dinners, serve on a committee, learn Scripture forward and backward, and even say a few amens on a Sunday when the pastor was extremely good.

After she was accepted and the bait was swallowed, she began to gossip and spread lies in a very subtle and convincing way. She would go to the people who she knew had a problem with gossiping and ask for prayer. She would say, "We need to pray about a very real problem that we have to keep quiet. Elder Jones was seen the other evening at a motel with a young woman who wasn't his wife." You can't imagine where that went. The truth of the matter was that Elder Jones stopped at a light in front of a motel with a young lady in his car who was not his wife, but his daughter.

She went from church to church spreading lies and causing trouble until one day she met a missionary who had dealt with this problem before in the mission field. He didn't sugarcoat the problem; he hit it head on. From the statements that had been made, he knew someone had to be lying. He explained that one of the characteristics of a true believer should be to always tell the truth. (While positionally we children of God are able to attain this goal through sanctification, we are still progressively growing in holiness, fighting against the old, natural man. Still we are the only persons able to tell the truth due to the power of God over sin.)

He prayed out loud with everyone present and bound her to tell the truth. From that point on, she was on a course of destruction. The power of Christ evidenced itself in the hearts of the believers who were willing to come together and grab the problem by the throat. It turns out that not only was the infiltrator a Satanist, she was an active member in a number of ungodly life-styles, including lesbianism. Today, Sharon Kuhn is married with children, has a ministry called Lifeline, and speaks nationwide on the subject of escape from satanism.

I challenge all pastors, who fall in the category of those

who know least about satanism, the occult, and witchcraft, to better educate themselves on the matter, beginning with reading what the Bible says about it. Author Dr. Mark Bubeck says in the preface of Dr. Fred Dickason's book, *Demon Possession and the Christian*:

> When the Lord first led me into a study of spiritual warfare, I was chagrined by the lack of preparation I had received through my academic training. Though having graduated from Bible college and seminary, my understanding of the believer's warfare with Satan's kingdom was almost nonexistent. I have discovered that I was not alone. . . . Pastoral leadership in our country is equally lacking in training and understanding of the believer's warfare.[1]

Dr. Dickason himself is grateful that a number of seminaries are now beginning to address the problem in required coursework. The easiest avenue for Satan's destruction of all of God's handiwork—his goal—is down the aisle of a church, particularly in the midst of an altar call. I would hope that those prone to sensationalism would not take this as an endorsement to point out demons behind every disagreement within the church or any person simply struggling with the walk of Christianity. The church can be the worst enemy a satanic group could have, or the amenable.

One of the saddest cases involving Satan's use of God's house as his playground was a recent investigation in Miami, Florida. After appearing as a guest on "Focus on the Family" in April 1991, I received several phone calls and letters pertaining to my work. I was asked to look into cases all over the country involving satanism, the occult, and witchcraft. In one week's time, I had no less than one hundred calls. One of the many cases I was called upon was a case in South Dade County surrounding the alleged activities of a fifteen-year-old boy named Bobby Finje (pronounced "Feen-yay"). Bobby was charged with sexually molesting twenty-one children in a satanic ritual in a church nursery.

I was contacted by Grady Moss, a representative of several families that had children who were sexually molested at the church. I could hear the sincerity in his voice, and his feeling of fair play was evident immediately in that one conversation. He explained that most of the families had heard me on "Focus," and they hoped that I could help them in some way. He explained further that several of the children were examined and found to have been sexually molested. The children had all pointed out Bobby as the one responsible, saying also that he had told them that there was no God, that Jesus was dead, and that Satan was their father.

Grady Moss mailed to me several newspaper articles and news videos from Miami to bring me up to speed on the development of the case. Through all this, not once did Grady get angry at Bobby or disparage his name. Quite the contrary, he said, "We would like you to look into this to see if it is true. If it is, we would like to see him prosecuted. If not, we would like to get to the bottom of this."

To me, this was a wonderful Christian witness on his part. I spoke to several other families in Miami who were involved in the case. Most of them had the same attitude as Grady and Stephanie Moss. Only a small number of these families showed a bitterness and anger. After speaking to Tony and Melissa Marin, and finding them to be the carbon copy of the Mosses in attitude, I decided to go to Miami to take the case.

We met at the Marins' home in Country Walk, a suburb in South Dade County by Kendall. They gathered as many of the families of the victims as possible. Before any introductions were made, we bowed in prayer and asked the Lord to oversee our meeting, guide our words and thoughts, and above all, if there was any bitterness and anger in the room, to rid us of it all.

After the introductions, I began by saying, "I can't say I know how you feel, because I don't. I have never had a child sexually molested. But God knows! And that's all that counts. 'Surely He has borne our griefs and carried our sorrows,' says the prophet Isaiah [Isa. 53:4]. However much you hurt, he hurts that much more, because these children belong to Him. They are only on loan to us while they are here on earth."

We had a very productive meeting with everyone giving input. I did not want to come across as someone who had all the answers, but as one who had handled this kind of case before, and more importantly, one who would call upon the Lord to guide our path. At the close of the meeting, one woman who had sat very still all evening, appearing nervous and a bit fidgety, finally spoke up at my coaxing. I asked her if there was something she wanted to share. She blurted out, "I can't help it, I'm mad, and bitter, and I'm going to stay that way until Bobby goes to prison." She got red-faced and started to cry. Hers was an example of the pain these parents had endured. I walked toward her and put a hand on her shoulder. I, too, began to cry. I very softly told her that scripture tells us it's okay to get angry, but in your anger, "do not sin; do not let the sun go down on your wrath" (Eph. 4:26).

Everyone in the room joined in and laid hands on her as we prayed to soften the heart of this child of God.

From the beginning there had been talk about satanic involvement, but no one seemed to be looking into it, according to the families and the news releases I saw on T.V. Not a new situation to me. Because the families were working closely with the state attorney's office and I was working with the families, it was just a matter of time before we joined forces and began sharing notes.

The police and the state attorney's office felt there was some kind of occult involvement, but to what degree was anybody's guess. According to the things I had seen and been told about, my guess was it was a form of voodoo. Given the geographical variable, more specifically, I guessed it was macumba.

Several stories were circulating regarding the possibility of satanic involvement, though none were proven. I feel very confident in my mind that at least some of these children were sexually molested, but I also believe there were some adults involved. I believe the goal was child pornography, and their attempt was foiled in the beginning. The satanic overtures, I believe, were a ruse.

My intentions for mentioning this case was not to go into the content or mechanics of it, but to show how a good Christian church was torn apart by a travesty such as this. Most of the victims' families left the church and had virtually no contact with the church and the people who stayed there. What a victory for Satan!

I did not have the pleasure of meeting the pastor or visiting one of the church's services, but I know the people there were grieving terribly. Lies, deceit, anger, bitterness, attacks on young children, and many more tricks and devices for manipulation were Satan's methods in dividing this body. I pray for this church often, as well as for the pastor and the individual members. The parts were broken and torn, which caused the whole to ache and groan. At the trial supporters of Bobby and family sat in the chairs behind him in the courtroom. Across the aisle were friends and family of the victims. These were brothers and sisters in Christ, and anger and bitterness remained as a wall to separate them from one another.

Every time I met with the families of the victims, we prayed for Bobby and his family and all those involved in any way. Our prayer was for the truth to be revealed. As of yet, in my opinion, that prayer remains to be answered.

Bobby was acquitted of the charges on 4 May 1991 after months of motions, denials, testimonies, and accusations. The attorneys in the case had filed so many motions, the case transcript was six feet thick. There were nine hundred witnesses' names entered for both the prosecution and defense. Jurors took notes to keep track of testimony.

An unusual thing happened in this case. The jury wrote a three-page letter to then-State Attorney Janet Reno, urging her to have another look at the case, stating that they felt something did happen to the kids, but the jury was duty bound to vote acquittal given the lack of evidence. Portions of the 9 May 1991 letter appear below:

> . . . His Honor's instructions as we began to deliberate, clearly stated that we are to presumed [*sic*] the defendant's innocence up to and until the State has proved otherwise beyond and to the exclusion of a reasonable doubt. It was our keeping with these instructions that led us to our verdict. . . .

> It is important . . . to note that though we believe something did happen to the two children in question, what and by whom was not certain beyond and to the exclusion of a reasonable doubt. And since, as stated

earlier, our task was not to prove the defendant innocence but rather his guilt beyond such a doubt, we had no choice, in following the instructions of His Honor, but to return with a verdict of not guilty.

Furthermore, we subscribed to the notion that there may have been more to this case than we were allowed to see and hear. However, no other charges, to our knowledge and at the time of our deliberations, had been filed. As such, our verdict could not be based upon our suspicions but solely upon the facts in evidence as we were allowed to review. However, we encourage the State's Attorney's Office to pursue with an appropriate investigation and file additional charges as deemed appropriate.

We would further like to express our sincere empathy towards the parents of the two children involved in this case. As being understandably disappointed with the verdict, we can only hope that if they are to blame anyone they blame the faulty system currently in place in the handling of these cases and not with we the jury.

It is our hope that this case will lay the foundation upon which a set of policies and guidelines are built. So that when cases of abuse, especially child abuse, are alleged, the programs in place will allow for appropriate questioning and investigation by the police, physicians and child psychologist [sic] so as to drastically reduce the chances of conflicting testimony and charges of contamination that can and will raise reasonable doubt.

We understand that a portion of the general public views our verdict as wrong. Understand that we were not privies to all information concerning this case. Furthermore, the general public received its information from the press in the form of a one minute opinionated nightly news segment. We, on the other hand, based our verdict on the law, and after listening to and reviewing the hours upon hours of testimony on a daily basis for almost four months. Consequently, our verdict stands. Sincerely, We The Jurors, State of Florida vs. Bobby Finje

Taking into consideration the thoughts of this jury—that something could have been done to more effectively bring a suspect to conviction—and the theory put forth by Dr. North as stated at the beginning of chapter 4, there is hope that much of the attempts made by the devil can be thwarted. The key here, however, is not whether he can be stopped, but whether those who are the only ones capable of accomplishing such a mission—believers—are willing to take up the challenge.

Joining Forces against an Already Defeated Enemy

In Scripture the visitation of an angel is always alarming; it has to begin by saying, "Fear not." The Victorian angel looks as if it were going to say, "There, there."—C.S. Lewis, *The Screwtape Letters*, preface.

Have mercy upon me, O God, according to Your lovingkindness: according unto the multitude of Your tender mercies, blot out my transgressions. Wash me thoroughly from my iniquity, and cleanse me from my sin. For I acknowledge my transgressions, and my sin is always before me. Against You, You only, have I sinned, and done this evil in Your sight—that You may be found just when You speak, and be blameless when You judge. (Ps. 51:1-4)

Specializing in criminal investigations is bad enough, but when you do nothing but homicide, narcotics, and ritual killings, you've pretty much made your choice of bedfellows. Usually, they are the kind that play for keeps. Unfortunately, with the high exposure I've had all these years, it is not surprising that I would average about three hospital visits per year. The moment you drop your guard, it happens.

A friend of mine worked as a teller at a bank where one of my businesses had an account. I always looked forward to chatting with her when I stopped in, but I found a sorry sight one day. She was sporting a black eye and a bruised face hidden behind a pair of sunglasses. I mentioned that black and blue were not her colors and that all the make-up was not very becoming. She burst into tears and said she'd been meaning to give me a call. Very quietly she informed me that her boyfriend had done this to her and that it was not the first time. She also added, "It's okay, because I had it coming this time."

I did not look surprised because I had seen this sort of thing many times before. I waited for her to explain why she deserved the beating. The stories alter only slightly from case to case. In the end, it's the same. The woman who ends up in an abusive relationship stays there because she believes somehow the beatings are justified. She never reports her husband (or boyfriend) because, "I don't want to get him in trouble; I love him."

My friend's story didn't break the pattern. The house was dirty, she hadn't done the grocery shopping, and most of all, dinner was not ready before he had to go to the baseball game. I assumed then that they had been living together.

Before I chided her for her ideas and assured her that nothing she does gives any man license to thrash her, I took advantage of the moment to pass along to her God's thoughts about the whole situation. Domestic abuse is just one of the things I have against an unmarried couple living together. If a man doesn't have enough respect for a woman to marry her, what would keep him from beating her up? I asked her what she was going to do about it.

"Nothing," she said. "If I report him to the police, he'll get in trouble. I love him too much to do that."

There it was. I explained that he had a sickness and that it would not get any better unless something was done now. I got permission to have a "talk" with him. It's hard to believe that this even goes on, much less that it happens more often than we care to admit. And it's more than just the poor, disadvantaged women of the inner city or the "backwards" rural towns. My friend is an example of how it can happen in the midst of sophistication and culture. She worked in a very professional atmosphere, dressed well, and was thought to be quite self-reliant.

I waited a few days to visit her boyfriend. I reasoned that this was not a high priority case, which turned out to be my first mistake. My purpose for seeing this young man was to let him know that someone was watching and if anything ever happened to her, we would know where to look. After a few days, I paid him a visit.

It was a hot summer day and the front door and windows were open when I arrived shortly after I knew he was due home from work. Heavy metal music was blaring from the house—it could be heard two blocks away. As I approached the front door, I paused to look around. That was my second mistake. I was about five feet away from the front porch looking off to my left when a young man in his late twenties, wearing a baseball uniform, burst out of the front door wielding a baseball bat.

I turned just in time to see the bat coming at my head from my right side. He was swinging for the fence. I flung my right arm up in time to block my head from the full impact of his swing. He hit me with so much force that he knocked me to my left about six feet. I grew dizzy and weak in the knees. He wound up again for another home-run.

I charged him with what little strength I had left, but he still managed to crack three ribs on my right side. I got him on the ground and gave him a stunning chop to the left temple. He rolled over on all fours as I grabbed the bat and swung hard enough to break the left arm first, then the right arm. A front snap kick to the ribs destroyed all his desire to fight.

With all the grace and nonchalance I could muster, I walked the short distance to my car. He rolled over to watch. I didn't want to give him the satisfaction of knowing that he had hurt me.

I drove myself to the emergency room at the local hospi-

tal, trying to figure out what had gone wrong. I found out
later that my friend had told her boyfriend that she had spoken to me. He was waiting. The pain was so intense on my way
to the hospital that I didn't even realize that I could not see
with my right eye. Besides three broken ribs, internal bleed-
ing, concussion, and a bruised arm and hand, my right eye
had been turned so far into my nose that the doctor could
only see the white part of my eye.

The most difficult thing to do was to call my daughter and
tell her what had happened. Equally painful was the realiza-
tion of what I had done: I had broken my promise. I knew
God was not happy about this, and neither was I. The scripture says:

> Walk prudently when you go to the house of God; and
> draw near to hear rather than to give the sacrifice of
> fools, for they do not know that they do evil. Do not be
> rash with your mouth, and let not your heart utter
> anything hastily before God. For God is in heaven, and
> you on the earth; therefore let your words be few. For
> a dream comes through much activity, and a fool's
> voice is known by his many words. When you make a
> vow to God, do not delay to pay it; for He has no
> pleasure in fools. Pay what you have vowed—better not
> to vow than to vow and not pay. (Ecc. 5:1-5)

My promise to God was that I would never again take a life
or injure someone unless it was in self-defense. I had not kept
my promise; I had gone beyond self-defense. No one else
knew, but God knew, and that was the source of my real pain.
I was as a fool before my God.

The sobs came, and the tears flowed. I dared not pity
myself; these were tears of true hurt and remorse for grieving
the Holy Spirit. I needed to do business with God. I know of
no other prayer that more eloquently describes the remorse of
man than the one that David prayed, Psalm 51. So I prayed:

> Create in me a clean heart, O God, and renew a stead-
> fast spirit within me. Do not cast me away from Your
> presence, and do not take Your holy spirit from me.
> Restore to me the joy of Your salvation, and uphold me
> by Your generous spirit. . . . The sacrifices of God are a

broken spirit, a broken and a contrite heart—these, O
God, You will not despise. (Ps. 51:10-12,17)

Several years ago, I got in the habit of praying on my
knees whenever possible—a position I sought when I knew I
needed to draw near to God. A hospital bed is not the place
to get on your knees, especially when you have an I.V. in your
arm. I raised the head of the bed as far as it could go and tried
to turn over on my knees. I was very thankful that I was in a
private room. Had someone captured this scene on film, it
could have passed for a take-out of an Inspector Clouseau
movie or an entry on "America's Funniest Home Videos".

Over the rail I went, knocking down the table and ripping
out the I.V. I landed on my head and shoulder, which didn't
do my ribs a lot of good. I got what I wanted; I was on my
knees. When the nurses came in and asked me what I was
doing, "Praying," I said through clenched teeth. Then I rolled
up into a fetal position.

It was such an embarrassing situation, that I never did tell
anyone about it, only that I had fallen out of bed. God has a
way of bringing our foolishness back to ourselves.

One evening about two months later, I was grocery shopping when I noticed a young man sitting on a bench just
inside the supermarket front door. I noticed that he had both
arms in casts with a brace under each arm going to his waist.
He also had a walking cast on one leg. As I got closer, I could
see that he was the same young man who tried to knock me
into the cheap seats.

When he saw me, his eyes got as big as saucers, and I
could see fear on his face. I began to say in a very slow and
quiet voice, "I would like to apologize for . . . ", and he got
up and hobbled away as fast as he could down the dog food
aisle. I yelled out in a voice loud enough to cause everyone to
turn and look at me, "I'm sorry!"

I found out that my friend went back to him for a few
months, then when she saw that the relationship wasn't going
to get any better, she severed the ties.

This is similar to another case, though clearly with elements less humorous, that I handled for my church. My pastor
contacted me about the daughter of a family in the congrega-

tion. She was living with her boyfriend who constantly beat her up. I started to visit regularly, stopping by every day. The third time I was there, her boyfriend came running into the house, breaking down the glass door, thinking she had another man in there. He ran right over to her and started striking her all over her face and shoulders. She was screaming and crying.

I was in the basement and heard all the commotion. When I got to the top of the stairs I saw her sitting on the floor and him hitting her over the head. I grabbed him and got a few punches in as I dragged him to the front door, kicking tail until he was out the door. I told him if he ever came back and tried that again, he'd find himself facing a .45 right between the running lights.

Says Deuteronomy 28:45-47:

> Moreover all these curses shall come upon you and pursue and overtake you, until you are destroyed, because you did not obey the voice of the Lord your God, to keep His commandments and His statutes which He commanded you. And they shall be upon you for a sign and a wonder, and on your descendants forever because you did not serve the Lord your God with joy and gladness of heart, for the abundance of everything.

It's easy to dismiss the words of the law of the Old Testament and claim that they are not for this period, commonly referred to by some theological circles as the age of grace. I am not a theologian, and I do not care to engage in a discussion about the appropriateness of scripture to any one time or place. To me, all the scriptures are the word of God, including the law.

I have seen over and over again the ramifications of violating the law of God. The sphere of disobedience widens and widens, blotting out access to the blessings of the Lord. These young women acted in disrespect before God's law, and they experienced the outcome of placing themselves outside the realm of God's blessings: abuse from their live-in boyfriends. Lesson one in doing battle against the wiles of Satan: Obey God's law.

> For I am not ashamed of the gospel of Christ, for it is
> the power of God to salvation for everyone who be-
> lieves. (Rom. 1:16)

I encourage parents to beginning praying continuously
that a hedge of protection be built around their children.
Hedge planting, though, can take many forms. Know your
children: where are they, what are they doing, who are their
friends? Love them, don't aggravate them, as the scriptures
admonish, but equally important, don't spoil them.

Young people who are drawn into rebellious behavior are
in search of something, whether it's the lure of a satanic
group, or the boys who are bound by drug addiction, or the
young ladies seeking love outside of marriage. They've got an
idea that somewhere out there is the magic formula to inject
perks into an otherwise confusing, dull, uninspired life. They
need to see that there is no hope in any kind of magic, that
reality and truth are the only answers. But how are they to
know that unless you show it to them. Everyday the reality and
truth will grow, building block upon building block, as they
see you involved in their lives, and them involved in yours.

I don't know how to say this without sounding sanctimo-
nious, but the straightest path to the heart of the matter of
satanism, the occult, or witchcraft is through Christ, and the
only way to know Him is to know His Word. Only with the
spiritual eyes inherited through sonship with Jesus can we
detect the workings of the enemy. A spy can't be a spy if he
can't see.

> But the natural man does not receive the things of the
> Spirit of God: for they are foolishness to him; nor can
> he know them, because they are spiritually discerned.
> But he who is spiritual judges all things, yet he himself
> is rightly judged by no one. (1 Cor. 2:14-15)

If I could draw a flow chart to show the development of
understanding law enforcement authorities have shown toward things of the darkness over the years, it would depict a
constant upward turn beginning at the left end of the chart
and rising to a peak at the right end. I am forever amused by
the contrast between the attitudes of the past and the attitudes

of the present. They actually put out a manual now! These are the very same people who whispered "wacko" under their breath as I walked into a room.

They still hesitate to give me any credit for any assistance I provide on a case, and they resent any hints that they have not handled the issue properly. They don't appreciate having egg on their faces. But that's okay. Just knowing that now they consider the element viable is enough satisfaction for me.

Many spies have offered to help me through the years, and I've met many interesting people in my work, from all walks of life. I have been fortunate enough to have met some very well known people and celebrities.

I was called in by the Vanderbilts of New York, specifically Cornelia Vanderbilt, daughter of Cornelius and sister of Gloria. There had been a breaking and entering at their home in Sun Valley, Idaho, and an intricate ornament designed by Tiffany's in 1870 was stolen. The insurance company asked me to retrieve the 300,000-dollar-plus item. I made several trips there during ski season and ran into Robert Redford and Barbra Streisand. They strolled into the dining room of the lodge where I was staying and sat down for their own impromptu piano concert. An enjoyable conversation developed before the tourists caught on and chased them away.

Two of the most impressionable friendships I've made since I've gotten involved in this work have been those I have the pleasure of enjoying with Christian counselor Dr. James Dobson and author Frank Peretti. Both have had a great deal of influence on the Christian community in convincing them of the severity of the problem of spiritual warfare and how to go about doing battle.

The reason for meeting these people are varied. They have needed my services for one reason or another. In some cases, the reasons were trivial to me, but monumental to them. In others, the need was true and necessary. The greater the need, the easier it is for me to convince them of their need for Christ. To me, that's what it's all about. If we believers have to sit and think of when the last time was that we witnessed for Christ, we're not doing our job. The scripture says "Go ye therefore into all the world and preach the gospel." That does not mean just pastors, evangelists, Sunday School teachers, etc., but all of us who have heard the "good news." If we don't, we are without excuse come judgment day.

You might think you are in a position or a job that does not allow you to witness to someone. I don't buy that. If God can use a private detective to witness to someone, he can use anyone. When I first started in this business, I didn't witness to a soul. I think it was because Christ was not first in my life— He wasn't even in my life! Now I can't even think of not telling my clients about God's love and how He directs our paths. Not once have I had negative feedback in their hour of need. Like the song says, God uses ordinary people just like you and me to do what He commands.

God uses earthen vessels to accomplish his will. He delights in doing the impossible with nothing. And that's what we are, nothing. Before God used Jacob, Jacob had to give up self. He called himself a worm, and I think that is what we must do. We must humble ourselves as worms before the Lord. The scripture informs us that in this humility we are to come to him boldly, to function with all the power of the Holy Spirit that has been placed within us to draw us to Him—a strange dichotomy to be sure, but it is consistent with the way God balances all of our interaction with Him: His sovereignty and my responsibility.

Have you truly desired to do some great work for God but have been held back because you feel you are nothing, or have nothing? Though we begin as worms, once transferred into His kingdom of righteousness, we are children of the Most High God. Don't give up! You're on the starting line of a great race that is about to begin if you hang in there. Fight the good fight, finish the race, keep the faith, but don't give up. Wouldn't it be great to have God say to you, "Well done my good and faithful servant"?

So many times in my life, during stress or at a time of loss, I have felt like giving up, but by the grace of God, through his holy scriptures, I have been able to hang on. Romans 8:18 says, "My present suffering cannot compare to the glory that awaits me if I endure." I know the fight seems impossible to win, and the race seems like it will never end, but remember, it's not your fight, and it's not your race! "Cast all your cares upon him, for he cares for you" (I Pet. 5:7). Once done, sit back and watch the Lord accomplish his will.

It is imperative to understand that we as Christians must continue to grow in knowledge about this spiritual warfare. We cannot rest now that the authorities recognize the problem, precisely because although they recognize it, they cannot analyze it with the same spiritual eyes that we possess. We know that Satan is our enemy; we know that in our salvation we have already gained victory over his edict of death, and we have knowledge of the outcome he is trying to evade: his ultimate banishment.

Long before the book of Revelations comes to an end, the devil, and death, and Hades (Hell) are all cast into the lake of fire to endure torment day and night forever and ever. Satan knows this is his end, though in all his wickedness, he still believes he can alter God's plan. Perhaps even more detestable to him are the last two chapters of the book, following immediately after the eternal sentencing of Satan. There God makes His promise to His followers for a new heaven and a new earth, and a seat for each of us at the marriage table of the Lamb.

It was over for Satan before it even began. He's been out of the game all this time. How do we still manage to give him a chance at bat? We believers have a responsibility to enter into the conflict prepared.

As Jessie Penn-Davis points out in *War on the Saints*, there is a specific difference between the way "the armored Christian" and "the non-armored Christian" approach spiritual warfare. The believer prepared for battle is characterized by the following: "armored with truth, righteousness of life, making and keeping peace, self-preservation (or, salvation) and control, faith as a shield, the scriptures in hand, and prayer without ceasing." In contrast, the non-armored believer displays "open to lies through ignorance, unrighteousness through ignorance, divisions and quarrels, reckless unwatchfulness, doubt and unbelief, relying on reason instead of God's Word, and relying on work without prayer."[1]

Let us take on these attributes of a warrior properly armed for battle.

—— * ———————————————————————————————

Epilogue

After unsuccessfully attempting to retire from detective work in 1989, Sal Dena is still doing investigations on a limited basis. Several calls come a week, but only the ones that pertain to satanism or the occult are considered. He has a problem with not being able to say no when people call in tears and have a genuine need.

Sal remarried in 1991, and he and his wife Barbara live in South Seattle with her two children, Mark and Laura. They enjoy remodeling their home, working in the vegetable garden and yard, and collecting antiques.

Sal is involved with a family business completely unrelated to detective work.

---- * --

Notes

Preface

[1]Mrs. Jessie Penn-Lewis, *War on the Saints* (Ft. Washington, PA: Christian Literature Crusade, 1977), 2.

[2]Dr. Gary North, *Unholy Spirits* (Ft. Worth, TX: Dominion Press, 1988), 3.

Chapter Two

[1]C.S. Lewis, *The Screwtape Letters* (Westwood, NJ: Barbour Books, 1990), 9.

[2]*American Heritage Dictionary*, 2d college ed., s.v. "satanism."

[3]Ibid., s.v. "occult."

[4]Ibid., s.v. "witch."

[5]Ibid., s.v. "witchcraft."

[6]From an interview with Dr. Fred Dickason on "Focus on the Family" (October-November 1992), Colorado Springs, CO.

[7]"Satanic and Occult Crimes: A Guide for Law Enforcement Personnel," Washington State Criminal Justice Training Commission (January 1988), 11.

[8]Ibid., 15.

[9]Dr. Judith Reisman, *Soft Porn Plays Hardball* (Lafayette, LA: Huntington House Publishers, 1991), 34.

[10]Ibid., 134.

[11]Ibid.

[12]Ibid., 135.

[13]Mrs. Jessie Penn-Lewis, *War on the Saints* (Ft. Washington, PA: Christian Literature Crusade, 1977), 1.

Chapter 3

[1]"Taylor's trail ended in Texas," *Highline Times* (28 May 1975): 1.

[2]William A. Clark and Michael Wendland, "The Gary Taylor trail broadens: 4 murder confessions are reported," *Detroit News* (25 May 1975).

[3]Ibid.

[4]William A. Clark, Charlie Cain, and Michael F. Wendland, "Sniper's movements traced," *Detroit News* (24 May 1975).

[5]Michael F. Wendland, "Sniper's movements across nation traced," *Detroit News* (30 May 1975).

[6]Clark and Wendland "Gary Taylor trail" (25 May 1975).

[7]Ibid.

Chapter 4

[1]Dr. Gary North, *Unholy Spirits* (Ft. Worth, TX: Dominion Press, 1988), 16.

[2]Ibid., 17.

[3]Ibid.

[4]Jonathan D. Maye, "Jackson reports to Reagan on progress of murder probe," *The Atlanta Journal* (24 June 1981): 22A.

Chapter 5

[1]*Encyclopedia Britannica*, 15th ed., s.v. "Rastafarian."

[2]"Atlanta Child Murders" Interim Report, G. Kelly Associates (December 1981), 6.

[3]"Atlanta Child Murders" Addendum, G. Kelly Associates (March 1982), 3.

[4]Micki Siegel, "Atlanta Postscript," *US Magazine* (30 March 1982): 15.

[5]Ibid., 16.

[6]"Atlanta Child Murders" Addendum, 8.

[7]Ibid., 1.

Chapter 6

[1]Panel discussion on "Focus on the Family" (October-November 1992), Colorado Springs, CO.

Chapter 9

[1]Dr. C. Fred Dickason, *Demon Possession and the Christian* (Wheaton, IL: Crossway Books, 1987), 10.

Chapter 10

[1]Mrs. Jessie Penn-Lewis, *War on the Saints* (Ft. Washington, PA: Christian Literature Crusade, 1977), 138.

More Good Books From
HUNTINGTON HOUSE PUBLISHERS

Gays & Guns
The Case against Homosexuals in the Military
by John Eidsmoe

The homosexual revolution seeks to overthrow the Laws of Nature. A Lieutenant Colonel in the United States Air Force Reserve, Dr. John Eidsmoe eloquently contends that admitting gays into the military would weaken the combat effectiveness of our armed forces. This cataclysmic step would also legitimize homosexuality, a lifestyle that most Americans know is wrong.

While echoing Cicero's assertion that "a sense of what is right is common to all mankind," Eidsmoe rationally defends his belief. There are laws that govern the universe, he reminds us. Laws that compel the earth to rotate on its axis, laws that govern the economy; and so there is also a moral law that governs man's nature. The violation of this moral law is physically, emotionally and spiritually destructive. It is destructive to both the individual and to the community of which he is a member.

ISBN Trade Paper 1-56384-043-X $7.99
ISBN Hardcover 1-56384-046-4 $14.99

Trojan Horse—
How the New Age Movement Infiltrates the Church
by Samantha Smith & Brenda Scott

New Age/Occult concepts and techniques are being introduced into all major denominations. The revolution is subtle, cumulative, and deadly. Through what door has this heresy entered the church? Authors Samantha Smith and Brenda Scott attempt to demonstrate that Madeleine L'Engle has been and continues to be a major New Age source of entry into the church. Because of her radical departure from traditional Christian theology, Madeleine L'Engle's writings have sparked a wave of controversy across the nation. She has been published and promoted by numerous magazines, including *Today's Christian Woman, Christianity Today* and others. The deception, unfortunately, has been so successful that otherwise discerning congregations and pastors have fallen into the snare that has been laid.

Sadly, many Christians are embracing the demonic doctrines of the New Age movement. Well hidden under "Christian" labels, occult practices, such as Zen meditation, altered states, divinations, out of body experiences, "discovering the Divine truth within" and others have defiled many. This book explores the depths of infiltration and discusses ways to combat it.

ISBN 1-56384-040-5 $9.99

A Jewish Conservative Looks at Pagan America
by Don Feder

With eloquence and insight that rival contemporary commentators and essayists of antiquity, Don Feder's pen finds his targets in the enemies of God, family, and American tradition and morality. Deftly . . . delightfully . . . the master allegorist and Titian with a typewriter brings clarity to the most complex sociological issues and invokes giggles and wry smiles from both followers and foes. Feder is Jewish to the core, and he finds in his Judaism no inconsistency with an American Judeo-Christian ethic. Questions of morality plague school administrators, district court judges, senators, congressmen, parents, and employers; they are wrestling for answers in a "changing world." Feder challenges this generation and directs inquirers to the original books of wisdom: the Torah and the Bible.

ISBN 1-56384-036-7 Trade Paper $9.99
ISBN 1-56384-037-5 Hardcover $19.99

Don't Touch That Dial: The Impact of the Media on Children and the Family
by Barbara Hattemer & Robert Showers

Men and women without any stake in the outcome of the war between the pornographers and our families have come to the qualified, professional agreement that media does have an effect on our children—an effect that is devastatingly significant. Highly respected researchers, psychologists, and sociologists join a bevy of pediatricians, district attorneys, parents, teachers, pastors, and community leaders—who have diligently remained true to the fight against pornographic media—in their latest comprehensive critique of the modern media establishment (i.e., film, television, print, art, curriculum).

ISBN 1-56384-032-4 Trade Paper $9.99
ISBN 1-56384-035-9 Hardcover $19.99

Political Correctness: The Cloning of the American Mind
by David Thibodaux, Ph.D.

The author, a professor of literature at the University of Southwestern Louisiana, confronts head on the movement that is now being called Political Correctness. Political correctness, says Thibodaux, "is an umbrella under which advocates of civil rights, gay and lesbian rights, feminism, and environmental causes have gathered." To incur the wrath of these groups, one only has to disagree with them on political, moral, or social issues. To express traditionally Western concepts in universities today can result in not only ostracism, but even suspension. (According to a recent "McNeil-Lehrer News Hour" report, one student was suspended for discussing the reality of the moral law with an avowed homosexual. He was reinstated only after he apologized.)

ISBN 1-56384-026-X Trade Paper $9.99

Subtle Serpent: New Age in the Classroom
by Darylann Whitemarsh & Bill Reisman

There is a new morality being taught to our children in public schools. Without the consent or even awareness of parents—educators and social engineers are aggressively introducing new moral codes to our children. In most instances, these new moral codes contradict traditional values. Darylann Whitemarsh (a 1989 Teacher of the Year recipient) and Bill Reisman (educator and expert on the occult) combine their knowledge to expose the deliberate madness occurring in our public schools.

ISBN 1-56384-016-2 $9.99

When the Wicked Seize a City
by Chuck & Donna McIlhenny with Frank York

A highly publicized lawsuit . . . a house fire-bombed in the night . . . the shatter of windows smashed by politically (and wickedly) motivated vandals cuts into the night. . . . All this because Chuck McIlhenny voiced God's condemnation of a behavior and life-style and protested the destruction of society that results from its practice. That behavior is homosexuality, and that life-style is the gay culture. This book explores: the rise of gay power and what it will mean if Christians do not organize and prepare for the battle.

ISBN 1-56384-024-3 $9.99

Loyal Opposition:
A Christian Response to the Clinton Agenda
by John Edismoe

The night before the November 1992 elections, a well-known evangelist claims to have had a dream. In this dream, he says, God told him that Bill Clinton would be elected President, and Christians should support his Presidency. **What are we to make of this?** Does it follow that, because God **allowed** Clinton to be President; therefore, God **wants** Clinton to be president? Does God **want** everything that God **allows**? Is it possible for an event to occur even though that event displeases God? **How do we stand firm in our opposition to the administration's proposals when those proposals contradict Biblical values?** And how do we organize and work effectively for constructive action to restore our nation to basic values?

ISBN 1-56384-044-8 $8.99

I Shot and Elephant in My Pajamas—
The Morrie Ryskind Story
by Morrie Ryskind with John H. M. Roberts

The Morrie Ryskind story is a classic American success story. The son of Russian Jewish immigrants, Ryskind went on to attend Columbia University and achieve legendary fame on Broadway and in Hollywood, win the Pulitzer Prize, and become a noted nationally syndicated columnist. Writing with his legendary theatrical collaborators George S. Kaufman and George and Ira Gershwin, their political satires had an enormous impact on the development of the musical comedy. In Hollywood, many classic films and four of the Marx Brothers' sublime romps—also bear the signatory stamp of genius—Morrie Ryskind.

Forced by his increasingly conservative views to abandon script-writing in Hollywood, Ryskind had the satisifcation near the end of his life to welcome into his home his old friend, the newly elected Presdent of the United States, Ronald Reagan.

In 1983, at the age of 89, Morrie Ryskind finally heeded the pleas of many friends and began work on his autobiography, workng in collaboration with John H. M. Roberts. *I Shot an Elephant in My Pajamas* is the result. You will find that this too-long delayed book was well worth the wait.

ISBN 1-56384-000-6 $12.99

The Extermination of Christianity
A Tyranny of Consensus
by Paul Schenck with Robert L. Schenck

Here is convincing evidence that a militant and secular coalition is using every available means to purge Christianity from of American landscape. if you a Christian, you might be shocked to discover that:

*Popular music, television, and motion pictures are consistently depicting you as a stooge, a hypocrite, a charlatan, a racist, an anti-Semite, or a con artist;

*You could be expelled from a public high school for giving Christian literature to a classmate;

*You could be arrested and jailed for praying on school grounds.

This book is a catalogue of anti-Christian propaganda—a record of persecution before it happens!

ISBN 1-56384-051-0 $9.99

Backlist/Best-sellers

Deadly Deception
by Jim Shaw & Tom McKenney

For the first time the 33 degree ritual is made public! Learn of the "secrets" and "deceptions" that are practiced daily around the world. Find out why Freemasonry teaches that it is the true religion, that all other religions are only corrupted and perverted forms of Freemasonry. If you know anyone in the Masonic movement, you must read this book.

ISBN 0-910311-54-4 $8.99

Exposing the AIDS Scandal
by Dr. Paul Cameron

Where do you turn when those who control the flow of information in this country withhold the truth? Why is the national media hiding facts from the public? Can AIDS be spread in ways we're not being told? Finally, a book that gives you a total account for the AIDS epidemic, and what steps can be taken to protect yourself. What you don't know can kill you!

ISBN 0-910311-52-8 $7.99

Hidden Dangers of the Rainbow
by Constance Cumbey

The first book to uncover and expose the New Age movement, this national #1 best-seller paved the way for all other books on the subject. It has become a giant in its category. This book provides the vivid expose of the New Age movement, which the author contends is dedicated to wiping out Christianity and establishing a one world order. This movement, a vast network of occult and pagan organizations, meets the tests of prophecy concerning the Antichrist.

ISBN 0-910311-03-X $9.99

Kinsey, Sex and Fraud:
The Indoctrination of a People
by Dr. Judith A. Reisman and Edward Eichel

Kinsey, Sex and Fraud describes the research of Alfred Kinsey which shaped Western society's beliefs and understanding of the nature of human sexuality. His unchallenged conclusions are taught at every level of education—elementary, high school and college—and quoted in textbooks as undisputed truth.

The authors clearly demonstrate that Kinsey's research involved illegal experimentations on several hundred children. The survey was carried out on a non-representative group of Americans, including disproportionately large numbers of sex offenders, prostitutes, prison inmates and exhibitionists.

ISBN 0-910311-20-X $10.99

"Soft Porn" Plays Hardball
by Dr. Judith A. Reisman

With amazing clarity, the author demonstrates that pornography imposes on society a view of women and children that encourages violence and sexual abuse. As crimes against women and children increase to alarming proportions, it's of paramount importance that we recognize the cause of this violence. Pornography should be held accountable for the havoc it has wreaked in our homes and our country.

ISBN 0-910311-65-X Trade Paper $8.99
ISBN 0-910311-92-7 Hardcover $16.95

ORDER THESE HUNTINGTON HOUSE BOOKS !

_____	America Betrayed—Marlin Maddoux	$6.99 _____
_____	Battle Plan: Equipping the Church for the 90s—Chris Stanton	7.99 _____
_____	*The Burning of a Strange Fire—Barney Fuller	9.99 _____
_____	*A Call to Manhood: In a Fatherless Society—David E. Long	9.99 _____
_____	*Christ Returns to the Soviets—Greg Gulley/Kim Parker	9.99 _____
_____	*Conservative, American, and Jewish—Jacob Neusner	9.99 _____
_____	Deadly Deception: Freemasonry—Tom McKenney	9.99 _____
_____	The Delicate Balance—John Zajac	8.99 _____
_____	Dinosaurs and the Bible—Dave Unfred	12.99 _____
_____	*Don't Touch That Dial—Barbara Hattemer & Robert Showers	9.99/19.99 _____
_____	En Route to Global Occupation—Gary Kah	9.99 _____
_____	*The Extermination of Christianity—Paul Schenck w/ Robert L. Schenck	9.99 _____
_____	Face the Wind—Gloria Delaney	9.99 _____
_____	*Gays & Guns—John Eidsmoe	7.99/14.99 _____
_____	*A Generation Betrayed—Randy Kirk	9.99 _____
_____	*Heresy Hunters—Jim Spencer	9.99 _____
_____	Hidden Dangers of the Rainbow—Constance Cumbey	9.99 _____
_____	*Hitler and the New Age—Bob Rosio	9.99 _____
_____	Inside the New Age Nightmare—Randall Baer	9.99 _____
_____	I Shot an Elephant in My Pajamas: The Morrie Ryskind Story—Morrie Ryskind/John Roberts	12.99 _____
_____	*A Jewish Conservative Looks at Pagan America—Don Feder	9.99/19.99 _____
_____	Journey Into Darkness—Stephen Arrington	9.99 _____
_____	Kinsey, Sex and Fraud—Dr. Judith A. Reisman/ Edward Eichel	11.99 _____
_____	*The Liberal Contradiction—Dale A. Berryhill	9.99 _____
_____	*Loyal Opposition—John Eidsmoe	8.99 _____
_____	New World Order—William T. Still	9.99 _____
_____	One Year to a College Degree—Lynette Long/Eileen Hershberger	9.99 _____
_____	Political Correctness—David Thibodaux	9.99 _____
_____	*Prescription Death—Dr. Reed Bell/Frank York	9.99 _____
_____	*Real Men—Dr. Harold Voth	9.99 _____
_____	*Spying on the Enemy's Camp—Sal Dena w/ Laura England	9.99 _____
_____	"Soft Porn" Plays Hardball—Dr. Judith A. Reisman	8.99/16.95 _____
_____	*Subtle Serpent—Darylann Whitemarsh & Bill Reisman	9.99 _____
_____	To Grow By Storybook Readers—Janet Friend	44.95 per set _____
_____	*Trojan Horse—Brenda Scott & Samantha Smith	9.99 _____
_____	Twisted Cross—Joseph Carr	9.99 _____
_____	*When the Wicked Seize a City—Chuck & Donna McIlhenny/Frank York	9.99 _____
_____	You Hit Like a Girl—Elsa Houtz & William J. Ferkile	9.99 _____

* _New Title_ **Total** _____
Shipping and Handling _____

AVAILABLE AT BOOKSTORES EVERYWHERE or order direct from:
Huntington House Publishers • P.O. Box 53788 • Lafayette, LA 70505
Send check/money order. For faster service use VISA/MASTERCARD
call toll-free 1-800-749-4009.

Add: Freight and handling, $3.50 for the first book ordered, and $.50 for each additional
book up to 5 books.

Enclosed is $_____ including postage.
VISA/MASTERCARD#_____ Exp. Date_____
Name_____ Phone: (   )_____
Address_____
City, State, Zip_____